ADVERSITY UNIVERSITY

A SPECIAL THANKS TO:
Wendy Chaney of NLBC and Robert Byers of Words that Work as well as the RUI editorial team led by Wendy Burks and assisted by Kay Niederwerfer and Joy Kingsbury. Special thanks to Rhonda Byers for her assistance on this project while very ill. Our ministry prays for your full recovery.
Design and Layout: Jeremy N. Jones

REFORMERS UNANIMOUS INTERNATIONAL

PO Box 15732, Rockford, IL 61132
Visit our website at www.reformu.com.
Printed in Canada
Cover design by Jeremy N. Jones

Dr. Paul A. Kingsbury, 1953-
Adversity University: The Fraternity for Eternity
Dr. Paul A. Kingsbury

ISBN 978-1-60702-968-7

ADVERSITY UNIVERSITY
THE FRATERNITY FOR ETERNITY

DR. PAUL A. KINGSBURY

Contents

DEDICATION

This book is affectionately dedicated to Janelle Marie Kingsbury. Janelle, whose name means "gift from God," is my fourth daughter and sixth child. She was born with cerebral palsy, and throughout her twenty years of life in our home and church family, "Nellie" has endured mental and physical adversity quite capably, and she has also been an instrument in the hand of our Lord to grow and develop our faith in God, both individually and collectively.

At her birth, in my immaturity, I was upset that God would give a handicapped child to a busy pastor and his wife and offspring. Her name seemed then to be grossly inappropriate. Oh my, I was terribly mistaken! Our family loves this girl and the God who so wisely and graciously selected our household for this difficult, but rewarding, assignment. Hebrews chapter twelve has helped us to see this grace more clearly.

INTRODUCTION

Welcome to Adversity University!

My son, Joel, graduated with a Masters' degree from a well-known and respected university. Following the ceremony during which he received his diploma, there was a reception (held inside an ivy covered building) in honor of the men and women who had successfully completed the courses required for graduation. There was music and food and drink, and it was all quite enjoyable for his mother and me to share in this occasion. However, our attention in the hall was diverted (nearly uncontrollably) from conversation with people to the interior walls of the reception room. These walls were covered with enormous, spectacularly painted portraits as well as biographical sketches and names embossed in gold leaf of former graduates of the institution. Their accomplishments were of such an extraordinary nature that their testimonies and likenesses were displayed for future students to admire and emulate. I remember thinking of the wisdom of this institution's leadership in sending their graduates into this room at this critical junction in their lives for inspiration and appreciation for that which they had received as students. This led me to meditate upon Hebrews chapter eleven...

Hebrews chapter eleven displays brief biographical sketches of sixteen men and women and "others" whom God wishes to honor for their successful completion of a lifelong educational program custom-designed by their heavenly Father. These men and women obediently, though not always perfectly, endured. Through their obedience, they received "a good report" (see Hebrews 11:39) and became great men and women of faith. Our wise Chancellor compels us to frequent this hall of fame for inspiration and appreciation of the adversity that we too must face and endure in order that we too might become people of great faith in God and obtain a good report.

Sadly, many believers have not grasped the truth that the moment they became a Christian, they were enrolled in what I call "Adversity University." Since then, every person, problem, pressure, and pain that they have experienced is a part of their educational development into greatness of faith. The very next chapter in Hebrews, chapter twelve, was written for our benefit that we might understand the "ins and outs" of our university training, and that we might endure and give our best efforts to successfully completing our courses, that we too might obtain a good report, be perfected (11:40), and please our Father (11:6). **The dropout statistics in God's University are staggering, and** many students **endure but are discouraged and disillusioned as a result of reality not** matching their **expectations of the Christian life.** These are the reasons for the writing of this book.

HEBREWS CHAPTER TWELVE IS THE STUDENT HANDBOOK FOR THE CHILD OF GOD

Hebrews chapter twelve must be carefully dissected and applied by each disciple (pupil, student, and learner) of Jesus Christ, lest they despise or faint at the chastening of the Lord as Hebrews 12:5 warns. Esau's life, mentioned in detail in verses 14 through 17, is our example for how our improper response to chastening will cause an individual to fail to see the grace of God This chapter in God's Word is the "Student Handbook" for the child of God. Failure to understand its teachings and consistently follow its guidelines is to guarantee our failure to obtain a good report and bring pleasure to our Creator and Saviour through maturing faith.

I regret that I failed to understand the principles of this Scripture earlier in my walk with God. Although I grew up in a Christian home and Bible-preaching church, and although I read and studied the Word of God consistently, the idea of a heavenly Father "chastening" me (as is the core emphasis in Hebrews chapter twelve), evoked in me only a mental picture of the leather belt which my earthly father thankfully used on my posterior when it was needed. This immature perception led to anger towards God when I had given Him my best; and yet, I experienced obvious, undeserved pain. If we do not understand the educational aspects of chastening, our logical conclusion when unfairness is experienced is that either God is not as powerful as we have been taught, or He is not the loving and just Father that we read of in the Bible.

What an eye-opening experience it is to discover that God's chastening is the *training* of a student and involves much more than punishment for disobedience. Chastening is corrective and instructive and not always given as a result of direct disregard for doing what we are told to do by the Lord. God chastens me through everyone and everything that He sends or allows to come into my life, so I might become like Abel, Enoch, Noah, and the many others we see in Hebrews chapter eleven.

No one ever grew and developed into greatness in any area of life without adversity. Therefore, God chastens us with adversity, not because He is necessarily angry with us (though at times I am certain that He is). His purposes for chastening are not to "vent" His frustration; but rather, they are to assist us in passing the next course, that we might advance in our faith and eventually become mature.

In this passage of Scripture, God uses athletics, our Saviour, and the mounts Sinai and Sion as illustrative examples. These illustrations, accompanied by the teaching of the Holy Spirit and the grace of God, have the power to adjust our attitude towards irritating and unjust individuals as well as difficult circumstances that frequently visit our lives. We can be inspired to accept our Father's will joyfully with endurance; knowing that He wants us to graduate with honors into His kingdom of Heaven for eternal service, having been useful to Him, while at the same time leaving behind a testimony worthy of inclusion into His hall of fame.

If you are saved, then you are a student in Adversity University. Using this book as a companion to the student handbook (Hebrews chapter twelve), it is my sincere prayer that you will complete your present classes, receive good grades, and advance to the next level in God's planned program for your spiritual, emotional, mental, and physical development. While in school, I admonish you to live by faith in Him and become active in Christian service for Him under His Under-Shepherd, the pastor of a New Testament Bible-believing church. You will be a bold witness to the unsaved around you who desperately need to see Christ in you as you respond to the adversities of your classes.

1. OBTAINING A GOOD REPORT

"And these all, having obtained a good report through faith, received not the promise: God having provided some better thing for us, that they without us should not be made perfect." —Hebrews 11:39-40

Special Note: *Please ensure that you have read the introduction to this book entitled, "Welcome to Adversity University." It is "required reading" for your first semester of classes as it will help you better understand how to properly navigate the halls (chapters) of this school of learning.*

First Alumni Directory

There are 1,189 chapters in the Bible, but no other chapter is quite like Hebrews chapter 11. I call this chapter the first Alumni Directory of Adversity University. The sixteen men and women named here, and the others who are spoken of, lived by faith and overcame the challenges that they faced. At the moment you were saved, God enrolled you in the "School of Adversity" to mold and shape your character, so that you would be like His Son. This course of study is designed to build your faith for you to live a life that is pleasing to God, for it is impossible to please Him without faith.

We know that when a person dies, he does not cease to exist. He either goes to a real Heaven or a real Hell. All of the men and women of faith who are mentioned in Hebrews 11 are now in Heaven. The Bible tells us that they all received a good report.

When I was in school, there were some kids in my classes who looked forward to report card days. They knew their parents were going to be happy with the grades they had received. (Didn't you just hate kids like that?) I remember having to call my parents during my freshman year at college and tell them about the grade I got in Greek class. It was <u>not</u> a good report. Similarly, Hebrews 11 and 12 is not only telling us about the lives of people who obtained a good report, but it also tells us how we can receive one as well. We can learn from the individuals listed in these chapters how we can also be men and women of great faith.

God's Evaluation

God's desire and design for every one of us is not simply that we get saved, but that we mature into perfect believers. Perfection in the context of Hebrews 11:40 is not being sinless; that is impossible. Instead it is spiritually speaking, referring to someone who has gone from infancy, through childhood, on to young adulthood, and now is a mature believer. This is supposed to be the natural progression of a believer.

Every day, I live with a reminder of what happens when someone does not develop properly. Our daughter Janelle is twenty years old, but she has the mind of a little child. She has grown physically, but her mental development did not follow the normal pattern. Every parent who has a child with a similar problem knows the heartache and difficulty that it brings. Yet there are many Christians, who, though they have been saved, have never developed into the mature believers God intends for them to be.

Salvation is about more than just getting saved; it is about changing our lives. God's plan is to take us and bring us to the place where we become like Jesus Christ. Maturing by faith begins with our commitment to obtaining a good report.

Now, what does it mean to obtain a good report? Hebrews 11:4

says, *"By faith Abel offered unto God a more excellent sacrifice than Cain, by which he obtained witness that he was righteous, God testifying of his gifts: and by it he being dead yet speaketh."* The phrase "obtained witness" is the same Greek word translated "good report" in Hebrews 11:39. When we come to the end of our lives, God is going to give us an evaluation of our work for Him. God testified and commended Abel for his way of life, because he had matured as a believer.

God looks at our lives and evaluates how we are doing. I know that when I reach the end of my race, I want to hear Jesus say, *"Well done, thou good and faithful servant:... enter thou into the joy of the Lord."* (Matthew 25:21) This thought drives me. It motivates me. It is a goal that I keep constantly in front of me. I do not want to be ashamed at His coming. I want to meet Him and hear Him say, "Paul Kingsbury, you did a good job; I'm well pleased with you." That is obtaining a good report.

But, Matthew 25 also tells us that getting a good report is not guaranteed. In verse 26, He says of another servant, "Thou wicked and slothful servant." Those are not words I want to hear. They were spoken to a man who took the opportunities and talents the Master had given him, and instead of using them, buried them in the ground. If we know that one day we will give an account of our lives and receive either a good report or a bad report, then how can we be sure of receiving the good report? The Bible tells us how in Hebrews 11:39-40.

Obtaining a Good Report

First, verse 39 says, *"And these all, having obtained a good report."* He is talking about the people mentioned previously in Hebrews 11 – men and women like Abel, Enoch, Noah, Abraham, Sarah, Isaac, Jacob, Joseph, Moses, Rahab, Gideon, Barrack, Sampson, David, Samuel, and the prophets. Many others are unnamed, but they slew lions, saw the dead raised to life, experienced pain and suffering, and yet the Bible says they all obtained a good report. Now, if you know much about these people, you know that they were human beings just like you and me. They did not always do things well. I have had people say to me, "Pastor, I could never obtain a good report because of what I did in my past." Abraham lied about his wife and fathered a child with her maid Hagar. Jacob was a liar and a deceiver. Moses murdered an Egyptian. David committed adultery and had Uriah murdered to cover it up.

No matter what has happened in your past, as long as you know Christ as your Savior, you can obtain a good report. None of us know how much time we have to live, but we can use that time to obtain God's testimony that we have pleased Him. There are those who passed through Adversity University before you did, and you are given this opportunity as well. They were frail. They were weak. They yielded to their flesh at times. They were disobedient. Yet, the Bible says they obtained a good report. No matter what you have done, no matter what you have failed to do, you can obtain a good report going forward. By God's grace, you can overcome adversity and graduate with honors.

Graduate with Honors

Notice next that verse 39 says, "These having obtained a good report through faith." It is critical to understand that a good report is obtained through faith, not through trying harder. Faith is bold obedience through depending upon God. When we consistently do what God says through faith, we receive His stamp of approval. We see an example of this in the life of Enoch. *"By faith Enoch was translated that he should not see death; and was not found, because God had translated him: for before his translation he had this testimony, (this is the same word again) that he pleased God."* (Hebrews 11:5) Enoch did not have to go through the valley of the shadow of death to get to Heaven.

Enoch walked with God from the time his son Methuselah was born. Enoch and God were on a walk one day as night was falling. The Lord said, "Well we're close to My house, why don't you come home with Me tonight?" Enoch went home, and no one on earth saw him again. When Enoch got to Heaven, the Father gave him a good report. Why did God say He was pleased with Enoch's life? It was because Enoch was a man of faith.

It is only through faith that you and I can please God. It is only through faith that you and I can receive a good report. Most of us would prefer to walk by sight. We want to see everything that is going to happen and how everything is going to work out, but God insists that we walk by faith. He does not tell us how we are going to make it; He simply tells us that we will and asks that we trust Him.

Passing the Course of Faith

God wants to give good reports. God wants to bless you and me, but He responds to our faith. We either live by faith, or we do not please Him. We see this clearly in what the Bible tells us about the heroes of the faith in verse 39, "And these all, having obtained a good report through faith, received not the promise." Now, we know that God always keeps His promises. But during the lifetime of these heroes of faith, they did not get to see the fulfillment of everything that was to come. The Messiah did not come in their lifetime. They never had the privilege of having a complete Bible like we do. Yet, they still lived by faith; and by faith, they obtained a good report. We have much more than they did. We know that Jesus came, lived, died, was buried, and rose again. We have the Word of God. We have the testimonies of the lives of those who have come before us. So, we have a much stronger basis on which to ground our faith.

If anybody ought to be able to live by faith and obtain a good report, it is you and I. Anyone who obtains a good report does so through living by faith. By trusting God to keep His promises through our times of adversity, we allow Him to finish His work of maturing us. We are incapable of perfecting ourselves. We need God to come alongside and bring us from a place of spiritual immaturity to a place of grown up faith. That is our course of study at Adversity University. It is designed to take us from the stage of spiritual little babies, where it is all about, "Me, my, mine, no, and gimme that." If we finish the course, we will come to the place of maturity in our lives where we fulfill God's purpose of growing to become more like His Son. That is what the Bible is talking about when it talks about being made perfect. That is what God wants to do in each one of our lives.

There will come a day when my daughter Janelle will be perfect. Both of her legs will be the same length. For the first time, she will be able to talk normally and run like other children. Knowing that one day she is going to be perfect helps give us the courage to keep working towards perfecting her now, despite the struggles. It is the same way with our spiritual lives. Knowing that one day we will be like Jesus Christ is an awesome, awesome thought. We will be made perfectly in His image. That is why Hebrews 12 was written—to teach us how God makes us perfect, in order that we might obtain a good report as we become men and women of great faith.

2. We Can Become Perfect

"And these all, having obtained a good report through faith, received not the promise: God having provided some better thing for us, that they without us should not be made perfect."—Hebrews 11:39-40

Spiritual Adulthood

We have been looking at the lives of extraordinary men and women of faith—the heroes whose life stories God has preserved for us in Hebrews 11. Yet, despite all that they accomplished for Him, and despite the fact that, because of their faith, they received a good report, they did not see the completion of the promises they received. They were not made perfect. However, God has given us the privilege of finishing what they started. If we are going to finish what they started, we are first going to have to be made perfect—growing spiritually to become complete and mature—ourselves.

Years ago, I was at a pastor's conference. While standing in an aisle in the auditorium during a break, I was surprised to be embraced from behind by a man. He gave me a big bear hug and then turned me around. I found myself face to face with a grown gentleman I had not seen since his teenage years. He was the kind of teenager that really improves the youth pastor's prayer life. He tested my patience and endurance. It was obvious at the time that he had no heart for the Lord. As he grew older, his attitude became more apparent and more bold. It was, "Well, I don't want to have anything to do with the things of the Lord." As soon as he could, he went his own way.

I had not seen him in twenty years. He could see the shock on my face as I said to him, "What are you doing here? Did you make a wrong turn?" What I found out was that he had made a right turn. He looked at me and said, "Pastor, I finally grew up." He was not talking about age; he was talking about his spiritual life. He had finally moved out of spiritual childhood, which is what the Bible means when it talks about being perfected. It does not mean being sinless; but rather it shows that we are maturing. When we are introduced to the patriarch Job, it is with these words, "There was a man in the land of Uz, whose name was Job; and that man was perfect and upright, and one that feared God, and eschewed (hated) evil." (Job 1:1)

Refining through Adversity

When gold is mined, the ore from which it is retrieved contains many impurities. These impurities need to be removed before the gold can be useful. The ore is placed under extreme heat until it melts. Through this refining, the dross comes to the surface, where it can be removed, and the gold can be perfected. This process has remained the same since Bible times. When Solomon built the temple, he used refined, perfected gold. (II Chronicles 4:21) In the same way, God is in the process of perfecting you and me. We are far more valuable to God than gold. His process of refining us and bringing us to spiritual maturity is called perfecting. From the moment a person becomes a believer, the person is enrolled in Adversity University for their perfecting; but the process is not automatic. We have a very serious and sobering responsibility in this matter of being perfected. This concept is a major topic in the book of Hebrews. In fact, perfection is so significant that it is mentioned twelve times in the book of Hebrews. Studying perfection, as it is spoken of in Hebrews, will help us understand our responsibility to grow up as believers.

Hebrews 2:9-10 says, "But we see Jesus, who was made a little lower than the angels for the suffering of death, crowned with glory and honour; that he by the grace of God should taste death for every man. For it became him, for whom are all things, and by whom are all things, in bringing many sons unto glory, to make the captain of their salvation perfect through sufferings." If we needed any further proof that our being made perfect is not talking about becoming sinless, here it is. Jesus was always perfect and sinless. (Hebrews 4:15) Though He was always good, he had to mature physically, emotionally, mentally, and spiritually. (Luke 2:52) Jesus endured adversity in His life, and it helped make Him completely mature as a man. Physical maturity is automatic in a healthy individual, but spiritual maturity is not. It requires a process that we must endure.

Perfect through Suffering

Jesus spent thirty years on earth being perfected (humanly speaking) for three years and six months of ministry. If this was necessary for the Son of God, then it is also going to be necessary for you and me. This can be discouraging, but it is absolutely true. The Son of God was made perfect through suffering. Now, I would prefer to learn this in school. I mean education is suffering enough. But God says, "No, that won't work. You need to experience adversity in your life. You need problems that are so big, you can't handle them by yourself." I have heard people say, "If God really loved me, I'd have smooth sailing every day." By the way, if you turn on your television, you can find some preachers who will tell you that. (You should not be listening to those guys!) The only way to become a good sailor is to learn how to sail through rough waters.

Hebrews 5:7-9 says, "Who (Christ) in the days of his flesh, when he had offered up prayers and supplications with strong crying and tears unto him that was able to save him from death, and was heard in that he feared. Though he were a Son, yet learned he obedience by the things which he suffered; And being made perfect, he became the author of eternal salvation unto all them that obey him." Again, here we see that Jesus had to grow and mature as a man before He was prepared for His ministry and His death on the cross. These verses tell us that we would have to forfeit our eternal life if the Son of God had not matured to become the author of our salvation. Now of course we are not anyone's savior, but our ministry for God is still significant. And, just as Jesus did, we have to grow and mature before we are ready to fulfill the ministry He has prepared for us. (Ephesians 2:10) God has people He wants you to reach, and He has lives He wants you to influence for Him. Are you grown up and prepared to fulfill His purpose?

Hebrews 6:1 says, "Therefore leaving the principles of the doctrine of Christ, let us go on unto perfection; not laying again the foundation of repentance from dead works, and of faith toward God." Since God never challenges us to a goal that cannot be reached, we know that everyone who receives Christ as Savior can be perfected; they can become mature. We can grow up in the Lord. We can change. Tomorrow does not have to be the same as yesterday. I am so glad that in my own life, this has proven to be true. I am also grateful that it is also true in the lives of people whom I care about, whom I love, and to whom I am trying to minister. What a delight it was to stand in the aisle of that church and hear a young man whom I did not have much hope for say, "Pastor, I grew up."

Beyond the Basics

Notice also the admonition that we are given in this passage. He says, "Not laying again the foundation of repentance from dead works and of faith toward God." First, we need to be sure who our Father is. There should not be any doubt or confusion about whether we are saved or not. We also need to go beyond the simple basics of the Christian life. We need to move past the foundations and the ABC's. Why doesn't everyone mature? Because the maturing process requires suffering. If we are not willing to suffer, then we are not going to grow. There is no way to shortcut the process.

Hebrews 7:11 says, "If therefore perfection were by the Levitical priesthood, (for under it the people received the law,) what further need was there that another priest (Jesus Christ) should rise after the order of Melchisedec, and not be called after the order of Aaron?" Perfection was not accomplished through the priesthood of Levi. Perfection is never going to be attained through any religious leader. A godly pastor is a great blessing, but he cannot make us spiritually mature believers.

We must cooperate with God by faith, endure adversity, and develop into spiritual adulthood.

I want my life to have a positive influence on other people. I thank God for the opportunities I have as pastor to help people grow in grace. I want my influence to motivate Christians to not be content with just being saved, but also to want to become like Jesus Christ. However, I realize it is not about me. The people I lead to the Lord are not Paul Kingsbury's converts. The people in my church are not my sheep. They are His sheep. I am simply the "under-shepherd." If we put our confidence in a person, no matter how wonderful he may be, we are going to be disappointed. There is only one Person who can bring us unto perfection, and His name is Jesus Christ. He is the only One.

School Rules

Hebrews 7:19 says, "For the law made nothing perfect, but the bringing in of a better hope did; by the which we draw nigh unto God." The law never did and never will make anyone perfect. There are some well-intentioned people who think, "If I can just put somebody under a rigid set of regulations, I can make them into a mature Christian." The author of Hebrews is debunking that lie. He is not saying that law or a set of rules are bad, because God would not have given us the law if it were not good. I am glad we have rules of the road instead of suggestions, aren't you? I want to know that the other driver is going to stop when the light is red. But the rules of the Christian life do not make us mature believers. The only person who can make us mature believers is Jesus Christ, and He does that through our personal relationship with Him.

This passage was written to Hebrew Christians who had lived under the law with 400 years of influence by Pharisees who focused all their attention on outward appearance instead of the heart. Their motto was, "Just get the look right, and everything will be all right." It is not about a look! It is about a life—a real life on the inside with Christ. That relationship is the only thing that brings us to spiritual maturity. The law made no one perfect, and no set of rules you keep will complete your maturity. Should we do right? Of course. However, we should never think that outward conformity will substitute for a right heart.

No Substitutions

Hebrews 9:9 says, "Which was a figure for the time then present, in which were offered both gifts and sacrifices, that could not make him that did the service perfect, as pertaining to the conscience." Not only are we not made perfect by religious leaders or by keeping the law, but we are also not made perfect by acts of service for God. Anyone can be active in church. But, that does not prove anything. Judas Iscariot served God, but he was not perfected in the process. He preached the

Gospel. He baptized converts. He walked with and served Jesus for more than three years...and he is in Hell today. Service is no substitute for a relationship with Jesus Christ.

Hebrews 9:11 says, "But Christ being come an high priest of good things to come, by a greater and more perfect tabernacle, not made with hands, that is to say, not of this building." Here is the key to the entire process: Christ is not only sufficient for our salvation, but He is also our sufficiency for spiritual growth and maturity. The earthly tabernacle that Moses built was just a picture—it was not perfect. However, Jesus is perfect in every way. He must receive all of the glory and honor for our spiritual growth.

Hebrews 10:1 says, "For the law having a shadow of good things to come, and not the very image of the things, can never with those sacrifices which they offered year by year continually make the comers thereunto perfect." The Christian life is a life of sacrifice. But, none of our giving brings us to maturity. In fact, Paul said, "And though I bestow all my goods to feed the poor, and though I give my body to be burned, and have not charity, it profiteth me nothing." (I Corinthians 13:3) If giving everything you have away and laying down your life as a martyr can be meaningless, then no amount of sacrifice will make you mature.

Hebrews 10:14 says, "For by one offering he hath perfected for ever them that are sanctified." When the Son of God died on Calvary's cross, He already foreknew every human being and everything about us. All of our sins, all of our iniquities, everything that all human beings have done wrong since Adam and Eve first sinned all the way down to the last sin, all of them were placed on the Son of God. He knew who had been saved during the times of the Old Testament, as well as those who would be saved in the future. In His sacrificial death, Jesus Christ perfected all believers forever. This is not something that is going to happen in the future. We have already been sanctified on the basis of His foreknowledge.

Christ said, "Paul Kingsbury is going to get saved the third Sunday night of March 1959; and right now, through my death, I am guaranteeing his perfection." I did not cooperate with Him for awhile. It does not take much maturity to get saved. I was just five years of age. It was not until I was seventeen years of age that I came to the point where I was willing to deny myself and take up the cross and follow Christ. You see, that took a measure of maturity before I even started the process of being perfected. But, Jesus guaranteed it while He was on the cross. My favorite verse in all the Bible is Philippians 1:6, "Being confident of this very thing, that he which hath begun a good work in you will perform it until the day of Jesus Christ."

Hebrews 12:22-23 says, "But ye are come unto mount Sion, and unto the city of the living God, the heavenly Jerusalem, and to an innumerable company of angels, To the general assembly and church of the firstborn, which are written in heaven, and to God the Judge of all, and to the spirits of just men made perfect." Who are these spirits of just men in Heaven? They are saints who are waiting for the resurrection of the body. It is a fact that when a saved person dies, their spirit departs the body and goes to Heaven. Paul said, "We are confident, I say, and willing rather to be absent from the body, and to be present with the Lord." (II Corinthians 5:8) And when we get that new body, it is going to be just as perfect as the spirit.

The Benediction

Hebrews 13:20-21 says, "Now the God of peace, that brought again from the dead our Lord Jesus, that great shepherd of the sheep, through the blood of the everlasting covenant, Make you perfect in every good work to do his will, working in you that which is well pleasing in his sight, through Jesus Christ; to whom be glory for ever and ever. Amen." As we have seen, the theme of perfection runs throughout the book of Hebrews. Now, at the end of the book, we find a benediction, reminding us one more time that God will make us perfect. Never give up! Keep pressing on the upward way. It may seem like you are taking two steps forward and three steps backward, but keep building a dynamic, personal relationship with the Lord. You will grow spiritually, and you will be perfected.

3. Somebody Is Watching You; What Do They See?

"Wherefore seeing we also are compassed about with so great a cloud of witnesses, let us lay aside every weight, and the sin which doth so easily beset us, and let us run with patience the race that is set before us." —Hebrews 12:1

Eyes of Faith

When you have children, sometimes it is difficult to find a quiet place where dad and mom may sit down and have a conversation. All the noise and interruptions can leave you looking for an oasis. I remember once Dianne and I sat down in the bedroom to talk, but the children really wanted our attention. One of the best pieces of advice I got when I first got married was to get a lock for the bedroom door. The kids knocked on the door, tried the door knob, and kept calling for attention.

When we told them to wait until we had finished our discussion, Jason, our oldest child, stuck his fingers under the door. He said, "My fingers see you!" Sometimes, you just can't get away. The truth is that someone is always watching us. In Hebrews 11, we saw the stories of the heroes of faith from the Old Testament. We saw the adversity, difficulty, and challenges that they faced. Now at the beginning of Hebrews 12, we are told about a great cloud of witnesses who are gathered around us. God wants you and me to know that they are watching us.

To see these witnesses, you have to look with the eyes of faith. There is an amazing transformation that takes place in an individual's life when he begins to walk by faith. That is the only way to live a life of obedience to God's revealed will. Faith lets us walk in His plan in spite of what we see, in spite of what we feel, and in spite of what our circumstances may be. The cloud of witnesses is assembled; and when we see them through faith, they help teach both young believers as well as those who are older in the Lord how to live a life of faith in obedience to God.

Spectators in the Coliseum

There is a great symbolism in the cloud of witnesses. It had great meaning to those who first read these words in the early church. Last year, our church was very gracious and sent Dianne and I on a cruise. One of the highlights of the trip for me was visiting the Coliseum in Rome. Construction on that great amphitheater started about 72 AD, and it was finished in 80 AD. Some fifty thousand people gathered to watch sporting events, gladiator battles, wild animal hunts, and executions. On occasion, they would even flood the arena and stage mock sea battles. For several hundred years, the Coliseum was the center of Rome's public life.

The Roman tradition of games and entertainment spread across the empire. Every major city had a coliseum or amphitheater. These were hugely popular, especially in the parts of the Roman Empire that had once been part of the Greek Empire with its tradition of the Olympics and athletic events. Often these arenas were the setting for persecution of Christians. Apparently, Paul was in that situation at least once. *"If after the manner of men I have fought with beasts at Ephesus, what advantageth it me, if the dead rise not? Let us eat and drink; for to morrow we die."* (I Corinthians 15:32)

As I stood there in Rome and looked at the famous remains of the Coliseum, I thought of the cloud of witnesses watching us, just as tens of thousands of spectators would watch the events during Roman times.

This is the picture being drawn for us here in Hebrews 12 with the great cloud—an amazing number of people. In this image, Earth is the arena; the floor of the Coliseum. Those witnesses who are sitting in the stands are those who have gone on before us. They have already fought the good fight and finished their courses. Now, they are in Heaven, and we are admonished in the text to remember that every day we are compassed about with that great cloud of witnesses.

Cheers of Motivation

The word translated witnesses here is the Greek word from which we get the English word martyr. These are people who had great faith and a public testimony that they believed in God, even to the point of death. Verse one of chapter twelve begins with "wherefore," meaning that on the basis of what we have seen in chapter 11—the stories of those great men and women of faith—we know who these witnesses sitting in Heaven are. Adam, Abel, Enoch, Noah, Abraham, Joseph, Moses...the list goes on and on. These are the spectators, those who have overcome adversity and learned its lessons; and those who have already run their races. They once were participants in the arena; and now today, they are watching and observing those of us who have followed them in the faith.

Why does the author of Hebrews tell us these heroes are watching us? He is using this as motivation. We are to recognize that these witnesses, or martyrs, were willing to lay down their lives for a great cause. Not all of them died for their faith, but they were willing to do so, and all of them did certainly live out their faith. It is important for us to remember that they are watching us. You only become a great man or woman of faith when you are willing to lay down your life. You see that is what Paul meant when he said, "*I die daily.*" (I Corinthians 15:31) I have crucified the flesh with its affections and lusts. (Galatians 5:24)

God wants us to be great people of faith, like those before us who voluntarily laid down their lives, their dreams, their plans, and their futures. He wants us to say, "My life is in your hands. I am glad You have saved me, and now I want to serve You. Whatever You have for me, I want Your will."

List of Spectators

The cloud of witnesses is not just Old Testament saints. I think about some of the great men and women of God who were so much a part of the founding and growth of North Love Baptist Church. I do not believe that they have lost interest in us just because they went to Heaven. They are part of that cloud. My mother is in Heaven. My father is in Heaven. Do they love and care about me less now than they did while they were alive? Of course not. With each passing week, more and more of those we love are joining that great host in the grandstand to witness us run our races, face our adversities, and follow our Savior. Sometimes, people ask me, "Preacher, do you really think the people who are in Heaven are aware of what is happening on planet Earth?" Yes, I believe that they do know, at least in a limited way, what is happening in our lives here on planet Earth.

And it came to pass, that the beggar died, and was carried by the angels into Abraham's bosom: the rich man also died, and was buried; And in hell he lift up his eyes, being in torments, and seeth Abraham afar off, and Lazarus in his bosom. And he cried, and said, Father Abraham, have mercy on me, and send Lazarus, that he may dip the tip of his finger in water, and cool my tongue; for I am tormented in this flame. But Abraham said, Son, remember that thou in thy lifetime receivedst thy good things, and likewise Lazarus evil things: but now he is comforted, and thou art tormented. (Luke 16:22-25)

Now, I realize that this story occurred prior to the death and resurrection of Christ. I believe that Heaven was opened up to the saved when Christ died on the cross. That is when He set the captives free and took them up to Heaven. (Ephesians 4:8) When an Old Testament saint died, they went to paradise instead of directly to Heaven. However, there is a principle being illustrated here. Abraham had been dead for many, many years. Yet, he was still aware of the events in the lives of Lazarus and the rich man. He seems to have offered a special comfort to Lazarus, probably because he had compassion on Lazarus for the miseries he had suffered in life. The rich man was also still aware of his five brothers, and he begged for help to spare them from joining him in Hell.

Adversity Awareness

I believe this same principle carries over today in both Heaven and Hell. So, there is awareness in Heaven of what is taking place on earth. The cloud of witnesses has a knowledge and awareness of our suffering, our successes, as well as our sins and selfishness. My friend, somebody is watching you today. The question is . . . what do they see? Do they see someone who is overcoming adversity and learning lessons, so that he is living unselfishly for Christ? Or, instead do they see someone who is living selfishly for his own interests?

Here is another look at what Heaven knows about life on earth. In Matthew 18:10, Jesus said, *"Take heed ye despise not one of these little ones; for I say unto you, That in heaven their angels do always behold the face of my Father which is in Heaven."* This verse teaches that when you and I were children, we were assigned angelic messengers from God. That is pretty astounding, isn't it? Now, I do not know how many angels you needed, but I probably needed a whole legion of angels to watch over me.

I was driving home one night in the middle of a snow storm with a car full of college students. It was late, and I fell asleep at the wheel. When I woke up, the car was all the way over on one side into the snow. The next moment, we were back on the highway. I still do not know how it happened, but I believe my angel (angels?) saved us. We were so scared that we stopped the car. My teeth were chattering. That old car had big rust holes on the side, and snow had filled the trunk we were so far off the road. Yet, none of us were hurt at all. I believe God looked down that night and said, "Son, I'm not done with you yet." The angels watch God's face for instructions to come and help us. I believe Heaven discusses what is happening on earth. We know that happened in the case of Job.

Adversary Awareness

Now there was a day when the sons of God came to present themselves before the LORD, and Satan came also among them. And the LORD said unto Satan, Whence comest thou? Then Satan answered the LORD, and said, From going to and fro in the earth, and from walking up and down in it. And the LORD said unto Satan, Hast thou considered my servant Job, that there is none like him in the earth, a perfect and an upright man, one that feareth God, and escheweth evil? Then Satan answered the LORD, and said, Doth Job fear God for nought? Hast not thou made an hedge about him, and about his house, and about all that he hath on every side? thou hast blessed the work of his hands, and his substance is increased in the land. (Job 1:6-10)

I do not know everything being discussed in Heaven. Obviously the Devil was either allowed or required to appear before God sometimes. But, Job's life was certainly the topic of conversation that day. Job did not know why the sudden adversity and the attacks of Satan came into his life; but I believe from the story, that those in Heaven were aware of what was happening to him and why it was happening. They understood the purpose of adversity in Job's life. Our loved ones who are in Heaven have a broader view of the attacks that are taking place in our lives than we do.

Some of the most famous parables Jesus told are found in Luke 15; the stories of the lost sheep, the lost coin, and the lost son. In verse 7, Jesus said, *"I say unto you, that likewise joy shall be in heaven over one sinner that repenteth, more than over ninety and nine just persons, which need no repentance."* Again, in verse 10, He said, *"Likewise, I say unto you, there is joy in the presence of the angels of God over one sinner that repententh."* People in Heaven know when someone gets right with God down here. Do you not think that family members up there get all excited about someone they love getting saved?

I don't think they see everything. I don't think they see wickedness or watch every time we sin. But as we have seen, the Bible teaches that people know in Heaven when we are suffering unfairly, when Satan is attacking us, when a little one is being neglected or abused, and when someone who has been sinning repents. It is a wonderful thing to know there are people watching and cheering for us from the heavenly coliseum. This is not just information for the brain; this is motivational. Knowing they are watching encourages me to live my life in obedience to the Lord; to give my best in the race.

Finish the Race

Who is watching you today? Which family members or loved ones are cheering you on? Who played a significant part in your spiritual life and is now in Heaven? Who did you help along the way who now is cheering for you to overcome adversity and win the race? Never forget the cloud of witnesses. I do not want my family members and others who are watching my race to be disappointed. I want them to see me with my running shoes on going full speed for the Lord.

They already know what the joys of Heaven are like. They know the reward for finishing the race. They know what you will miss if you don't run the race like you should. Do they see you having put off the weights, so you can run without hindrance? Do they see you suffering for doing right? Do they see you slacking off? Are they pleased with the way you are running the race, or are they embarrassed to admit they know who you are?

If you want to be a Hebrews 11 Christian, if you want to graduate from Adversity University, and if you want to be a great person of faith, then you need to remember the witnesses—those who are watching you run the race. One of the most famous moments in Olympic history happened in 1992 at the Barcelona Games. The British runner Derek Redmond was a favorite to win the gold medal in the 400 meter race. He had posted the fastest times in the first two rounds; but in the semifinal race, he tore his hamstring and fell to the track writhing in pain.

He made it to his feet, refusing help from the staff at the track. If a runner is helped in any way, they do not get credit for finishing the race—and Redmond wanted to finish even though his dream of a medal had vanished. Limping and struggling, he made his way around the track, but the pain was getting worse. But, Derek Redmond was not alone. His father was in the stands; and when he saw the agony of his son, he made his way to the infield. Brushing by the guards, he joined his son on the track. He placed Derek's arm around his shoulder and helped him to complete his race. Derek would not have made it had it not been for one special witness that day. Someone is watching you run your race today. What do they see?

4. LET US RUN THE RACE

"And these all, having obtained a good report through faith, received not the promise: God having provided some better thing for us, that they without us should not be made perfect. Wherefore seeing we also are compassed about with so great a cloud of witnesses, let us lay aside every weight, and the sin which doth so easily beset us, and let us run with patience the race that is set before us."

—Hebrews 11:39-12:1

Enrolled in School and in the Race

I have told you that Hebrews 12 is designed to show us how to grow in grace and faith, so that we can graduate from Adversity University with a good report. You were enrolled in this school on the day you were saved, and you will be in classes until God calls you home. In life, as we suffer various problems and adversities, we have the choice of giving up and quitting or continuing on in faith. The author of Hebrews refers to this as running the race. I was five years old when I received Jesus Christ as my personal Savior; and at that time, I had no idea about the race that would last for the rest of my life. But, I have been running it ever since.

When most of us think of long races, we think of the marathon. According to tradition, a Greek runner named Pheidippides ran from Marathon to Athens to bring news of the victory over Darius and the Persians. After running the twenty-six miles to bring his report, he supposedly collapsed and died. The marathon is long, but the really hardcore runners (the crazy ones) compete in an event called the extreme marathon. They run 156 miles—six marathons in six days. I do good to stay on the treadmill for thirty minutes! The Christian life is an endurance event, not a sprint. It is not about starting; it is about finishing.

Purpose of the Race

To understand God's purpose for enrolling us in Adversity University and placing us in the race, we need to understand what the analogy of the race is meant to convey. To do that, we need to look at Galatians 5:7. Paul wrote, *"Ye did run well; who did hinder you that ye should not obey the truth?"* Notice that he uses the past tense; Paul was writing people who had once been running, but they had dropped out. In Galatians, Paul is writing a group of churches that were not growing spiritually as God wanted them to grow. They had started well, but then they stopped. We see in this verse what running well symbolizes. When we obey the truth—when we do what the Bible says, we run well. When we stop obeying, we stop running. So, when Hebrews 12:1 says, "Let us run...the race," it is talking about living in obedience to the revealed will of God through His Word.

First, we see that **we run to obtain a good report**. We have seen already how we obtain the approval and testimony of God. Through faith we mature as we run the race and become men and women of extraordinary faith. Make no mistake; the idea of obtaining a good report also implies the possibility of obtaining a bad report. The day is coming when we will stand before the Lord to give an account of our lives. None of us know when that moment will be. We could hear the sound of the trumpet this very day. I want to be found running, and not walking, standing, or sitting when He comes. Running the race is not optional if we want a good report.

Next, **we run to be made perfect**. God wants us to grow up and shape up. My wife and I got married thirty-four years ago. I would hate for her to have to say, "Paul is the same as he was at twenty-one. He hasn't matured. He hasn't improved. Nothing has changed." I should be more like Jesus Christ today than I was years ago. God never gives us a calling that He does not enable us to fulfill. So, when He tells us to be perfect, it is possible for us to do just that. We can grow as believers. While it is not possible for us to be sinless, it is God's intention that we sin less and less and become more like Jesus Christ. That only happens if we accept the challenge to keep running the race. Athletes do not get in shape by watching videos of runners; they get in shape by running.

Hindrances of Excess Baggage

Third, **we run by laying aside every weight** that hinders us. Have you ever seen a runner in a race wearing a raincoat and boots? There is no rule against wearing raincoats or boots, but no serious athlete would wear them. Why? You cannot run well if you are weighted down. There are issues, there are relationships, there are activities, and there are attitudes that in and of themselves are not necessarily wrong, but they are still not helpful in running the race. An immature Christian says, "Well, if there's not a verse in the Bible that says specifically I can't do that, you can't prove it's wrong." Those little hindrances, those little weights will keep you from running the race unless you are willing to lay them aside.

Nothing that keeps you from running the race is worth holding on to, no matter how much you enjoy it. Often, people hold on to relationships, jobs, hobbies, or habits even though they know that they are being hindered because of them. They rationalize, excuse, and try to explain it away. That is very dangerous. Those weights do not just hinder us from running well; if we wear them long enough, they can force us to drop out of the race.

Fourth, **we run by laying aside sin**. The Bible is very specific here. It is not talking about sin in general; rather it is singular—one specific, besetting sin that you must lay aside. This sin is singular in nature, but it is habitual in practice. In other words, it is one that you struggle with again and again. Over time, your besetting sin can change. When I was in elementary school, it was absolutely imperative to me that I be accepted by my buddies. I smoked to fit in—once! One puff of a cigar cured me forever! And I will not even begin to describe the feeling that swallowing a wad of Redman chewing tobacco brings to your stomach. Again, one taste was all it took to keep me from ever doing that again. Why did I do it in the first place? Because peer pressure and gaining the acceptance of others was my biggest problem in those days. Now, I face other things. My besetting sin has changed over time. However, it is still there. Until I meet the Lord, there will always be a besetting sin that I must lay aside.

Other Participants in the Race

Fifth, we see that **we run with others**. The verse says, "Let us run." The Christian race is not an individual event. You should seek the company and companionship of runners. They can help and encourage you along the way. However, if someone refuses to run, it will be impossible for you to keep running and still remain in their company. Then you have to make a choice. Many who once were good runners in the Christian life are not running any longer because of someone else. I know some preachers who have sinned and destroyed their ministries. The sad thing is that often people in those churches stop running too. It is good to have encouragement and fellowship, but do not stop running just because someone else falls out of the race. Keep on!

Sixth, to succeed in this race, **we must run with patience.** The word here is similar to the word "endurance" in verse two, but it is more involved. It is not just gritting your teeth and hanging on; patience is enduring trials and struggles with a calm and cheerful spirit! That is impossible for man, but it is possible for a Spirit-filled Christian. Have you ever watched the runners in a marathon, especially toward the end of the race? They do not look to me like they are having a whole lot of fun. Their faces are strained, there is sweat pouring off their faces, but they continue to run. You do not see them stopping to complain about the course, or the weather, or the other runners. They are too busy running to gripe. They have a goal and a purpose that drives them on. And, as believers, we are to keep running the race with cheerful endurance.

The Marathon

Finally, **we run the race that is set before us.** There are two different Greek words for race that are used in different places in the New Testament.

The first is the word *stadion*, from which we get stadium. This is the common word for race that we find used most often in the Bible. The *stadion* was a course of six hundred feet, over which the racers would run. But as I have told you, the Christian life is not a sprint, it is a marathon, and that word would not fit here. Instead, the second Greek word for race, *agon*, is the one we find in Hebrews 12:1. I am sure I do not have to tell you what words we get from that in English! This is a long, grueling, painful, and difficult race—it is an agony to run. This word is not used often; and in fact, it is not translated as race any of the other times it is used. Looking at the five other places this word is used in Scripture will help us understand what God is telling us about the race that is set before us.

In Philippians 1, Paul was warning the church about those who would resist their efforts to preach the Gospel; and in verse 30, he said, "Having the same conflict which ye saw in me." This race is a battle—it is a conflict which we must endure. The word is translated conflict again in Colossians 2:1, where Paul said, "*I would that ye knew what great conflict I have for you.*" Paul also used the word twice in his letter to Timothy where it is translated as fight. Paul told Timothy to, "*Fight the good fight of faith*" in I Timothy 6:12. In his last epistle, he said, "*I have fought a good fight, I have finished my course, I have kept the faith.*" (II Timothy 4:7) Finally, it is used in I Thessalonians 2:2. Here, Paul is describing the opposition he had faced and the persecution he had endured when he said, "*we were bold to speak unto you the Gospel of God with much contention.*"

Race with Determination, or Drop Out

Our race is not the *stadion,* it is the *agon.* It is conflict. It is tension. It is the fighting. You will be exhausted. You will want to quit. You will get discouraged. You will think it is too hard, and you will want to give up. Run! Run with patience the race that is set before you. It does not matter what the other runners do. It does not matter what opposition you face. It does not matter how tired you are. You can still keep running. Isaiah 40:31 says, "*But they that wait upon the Lord shall renew their strength; they shall mount up with wings as eagles; they shall run, and not be weary; and they shall walk, and not faint.*"

When Dianne and I were teenagers, we were blessed to have two great spiritual leaders in our lives. They were runners in the Hebrews 12 sense of the word. They ran sacrificially. They had learned the Word and walked with God.

Though they had talents and could have made a lot more money in other fields, they chose the ministry so that they could lead God's people. They had a tremendous impact on our lives. Yet, sadly today, both of those men have dropped out of the race. Though they are still alive, they are just existing. No longer do they point others to Christ. No longer do they exhort and encourage God's people. What happened? A series of hurts that were not properly responded to led them to quit their race for the Lord. And, certainly, they are not alone.

I recently read a thesis that a man had written for his doctorate on the problem of burnout in the ministry. He had conducted surveys of dozens of former and current pastors, missionaries, and spiritual leaders from churches across America and around the world. These were all people who had worked diligently for the Lord. Every one of them faced difficult circumstances and problems in the ministry. Those who quit had one common thread. You could trace every burnout to a series of circumstances involving individuals who hurt them and hurt them and hurt them and hurt them. Eventually, they said, "I'm not going to be hurt like this any more." To escape the hurt, they dropped out of the race. In doing so, they forfeited a good report. They lost out on being made perfect. The great cloud of witnesses who were watching them was disappointed. They stopped running.

The fact that you have run well for a long time does not guarantee you will stay in the race. Paul said, *"I keep under* (literally that means to beat black and blue) *my body, and bring it into subjection: lest that by any means, when I have preached to others, I myself should be a castaway."* (I Corinthians 9:27) Paul was afraid of being disqualified. He forced himself to continue running. That is why he was able to tell Timothy that he finished his course. Do not allow pain, struggle, suffering, or conflict with others to cause you to drop out. Instead, focus your eyes on Jesus and keep running.

5. LOOKING UNTO JESUS

"Wherefore seeing we also are compassed about with so great a cloud of witnesses, let us lay aside every weight, and the sin which doth so easily beset us, and let us run with patience the race that is set before us, Looking unto Jesus the author and finisher of our faith; who for the joy that was set down before him endured the cross, despising the shame, and is set down at the right hand of the throne of God." —Hebrews 12:1&2

Focus on Him

I loved playing baseball when I was a boy. I remember learning how to pick out a bat. I had to find one that was the right length and weight. Then, I had to learn what to do with the bat. Over and over again, the coaches would tell me, "Paul, keep your eye on the ball." I would walk to the batters' box to face the pitcher, but there were so many other things happening at the same time. There were the players on the other team in the field. There were my teammates in the dugout. There were guys selling hot dogs and cokes in the stands. But, if I was not watching the pitcher, I was going to have a problem. And so the coaches kept telling me, "Keep your eye on the ball." That is the same idea we find in Hebrews 12:2 when it says, "Looking unto Jesus."

Do you remember the story of Peter walking on the water? Peter was one of those guys who talk before they think. It was late at night, and the disciples were in the boat. They were struggling with a storm;

and Jesus, who had stayed behind to pray, came walking to them on the water. The disciples freaked out, thinking they were seeing a ghost. When Jesus told them who He was, Peter said, "*Lord, if it be thou, bid me come unto thee on the water.*" (Matthew 14:28) Now, I do not think that is what I would have said, but that's what Peter said. And when Jesus said, "*Come,*" *Peter got out of the boat and started walking on the water. As long as Peter looked to Jesus, everything was fine.* "*But when he saw the wind boisterous, he was afraid; and beginning to sink, he cried, saying, Lord, save me.*" (Matthew 14:30) Why did Peter sink? He started looking at the storm instead of looking at Jesus.

The point is that we must focus. While we must be aware of our past, our focus needs to be on Jesus Christ. Our lives may be filled with problems and difficulties, but our focus must be on Him. Our futures may be unclear, but our focus should be fixed. Jesus is our only hope of success in running the race. This word "look" is an active, continuous, present-tense verb. Looking to Jesus is not a one-time thing. It is something we have to do every day, if we want to stay on track for Him. This verse gives us six specific portraits or descriptions of Christ that help us see Him clearly through the eyes of faith.

The Author and Finisher

First, **Jesus is the author of our faith**. The idea here is that He is the One who begins everything—not just our model for running the race, but the starter. He sets the race in motion when He saves us and places us into God's family. But, when we think of authors; most often, we think of books. Authors are all about words. If we try to write the story of our own lives, we will end up with fairy tales instead of a life of faith. Jesus wrote the stories of the men and women of extraordinary faith we find in Hebrews 11. The past chapters of your life may be bleak, but He can write new chapters for your future.

Second, **Jesus is the finisher of our faith**. He did not just start the race and leave us to flounder and struggle alone. Paul said, *"Being confident of this very thing, that he which hath begun a good work in you will perform (bring to an end) it until the day of Jesus Christ."* (Philippians 1:6) Jesus is not about just starting a race; He is the finisher. In John 17:4, in His prayer in the upper room, Jesus said to His Father, *"I have glorified thee on the earth: I have finished the work which thou gavest me to do."* On the cross, Jesus cried out *"It is finished"* (John 19:30), using the same root word we find here in Hebrews 12. He did not just run part of the race, He ran all the way to the finish line at Calvary. Because He finished His race, we can find the grace to finish ours. We each need Jesus to author and to finish our faith.

Years ago, my wife convinced me that I should build a new kitchen table for our family. She presented me with the plan she had ordered for a trestle table. On the front of the blueprint was a picture of a beautiful hardwood trestle table. I knew when I started the project that it was going to take a lot of work. It was not going to be done in a day, a week, or even a month. So, I took the picture from the instructions, enlarged it, and taped it over the bench in my shop. While I worked on the various steps of the instructions, I could keep my focus on the finished product—the beautiful trestle table in the picture and the smiling family sitting at the table. That picture helped me finish the task. There were a lot of long hours put into that table. There were times when I did not think it would ever get done. But, I kept looking at that picture. Then, one day, it was finally done! Keep your attention focused on the Finisher of your faith, and you will stay in the race.

Focus on the End Result

Third, **Jesus anticipated the joy that was set before Him**. This is so important. Jesus was suffering incredible physical pain on the cross. Even worse, He was taking our sins on Himself, and He was separated from the Father. There was no joy in what He was experiencing. But, there was a joy in what was to come that outweighed what He was going through. Jesus knew that He was doing the Father's will, so He kept running the race. Even as a twelve-year old boy, He told Mary, *"I must be about my Father's business."* He knew His purpose, and He knew what would result from His obedience. Do you know why people get discouraged and drop out of the race? It is because people who do not anticipate future blessing will not endure present suffering. Do not lose your focus on the reward that is waiting for you when you finish. The race is not forever. One day, I will step into joy in the presence of the Lord. That anticipation leads to the willingness to deny ourselves, take up our cross, and follow Jesus Christ our Savior.

Focus on Endurance, Not on Enjoyment

Fourth, **Jesus endured the cross**. He could have stopped the process at any moment. A simple request to His Father would have brought more than sixty thousand angels (the song isn't quite right when it says ten thousand angels—a legion was about five thousand soldiers, and Jesus said the Father would send "more than twelve") to His rescue. (Matthew 26:53) If we can get a clear view of Jesus Christ enduring the cross, we will appreciate His love for us in a new way. Many Christians seem to have personal enjoyment as their only goal in life. Jesus did not enjoy everything in His life. Life is not about enjoyment; it is about endurance. We endure our race the same way Jesus endured His—by focusing on what is waiting for us at the finish line.

Fifth, **Jesus despised the shame.** The cross was designed to be, not just a means of execution, but a slow, painful, and humiliating means of execution. Crucifixion was intended to be a warning and a deterrent to those who witnessed it. The thing that makes Jesus Christ unique is that He humbled Himself. *"And being found in fashion as a man, he humbled himself, and became obedient unto death, even the death of the cross."* (Philippians 2:8) Because He was already humbled, the shame of the cross did not mean anything to Him. Jesus was tortured, mocked, spit on, ridiculed, mistreated, and hung naked in public before thousands of people. He despised the shame.

The next time someone hurts your feelings, focus on Jesus. He despised the shame—literally it means He thought the shame was nothing. That does not mean it didn't hurt! There will be real pain and adversity in your life. People will criticize you and treat you unfairly. But you do not have to let it embarrass you to the point where you quit the race. Will it matter in eternity if someone put you down? That is why Jesus despised the shame; it did not compare to the joy that was set before Him. He loved you enough to go through all of that for you. In enduring the cross, He set an example that we can follow in running our race.

Crossing the Finish Line

Finally, **Jesus is seated at the right hand of the throne of God**. The race the Father laid out for Jesus to run is finished. He returned to Heaven; His suffering was over. There are days when our lives seem to be filled with pain and adversity that will never end. But there will come a day when we will finally go Home. Nothing that we have endured will compare to the joy of the reward that we will gain on that day. The Apostle Paul put it this way:

For which cause we faint not; but though our outward man perish, yet the inward man is renewed day by day. For our light affliction, which is but for a moment, worketh for us a far more exceeding and eternal weight of glory; While we look not at the things which are seen, but at the things which are not seen: for the things which are seen are temporal; but the things which are not seen are eternal. (II Corinthians 4:16-18)

When I first became the senior pastor at North Love Baptist Church, there were days when the pressures of the ministry were overwhelming. I was in my late 20's, and some days I just was not sure that I had what it took to lead a church. Often, I would go over to the school (across from where we lived then) and just walk. If you had asked me, I would have told you I was praying, but what I was really doing was griping to God. I remember one night my son Jason asked to go with me. As we walked together, I was burdened down with the problems of the ministry. Jason said, "Dad, I want to sing a song." Well, I sure didn't feel much like singing, but I said, "Go ahead." And Jason started singing:

> *My God is so big,*
> So strong and so mighty,
> *There's nothing my God cannot do.*

He did not know what I was going through, but he had the answer I needed! I was so focused on what was going on in my life and ministry, that I had forgotten my God was big enough to take care of every problem I had. Instead of looking around me, I needed to focus on Jesus. When you head out the door for your responsibilities for the day, look unto Jesus. When a problem comes up that you do not know how to handle, look unto Jesus. When friends turn their backs on you and people you count on let you down, look unto Jesus. When you do not see any way out of the adversity you are facing, look unto Jesus. In all the circumstances of life, look always to Christ. If you do, you will keep running, and you will be a winner.

6. CONSIDER HIM

"Wherefore seeing we also are compassed about with so great a cloud of witnesses, let us lay aside every weight, and the sin which doth so easily beset us, and let us run with patience the race that is set before us, Looking unto Jesus the author and finisher of our faith; who for the joy that was set down before him endured the cross, despising the shame, and is set down at the right hand of the throne of God. For consider him that endured such contradiction of sinners against himself, lest ye be wearied and faint in your minds."

–Hebrews 12:1-3

Become Meticulously Acquainted

If it were in our nature to live by faith, Hebrews 12 would not be necessary. Since it is not natural, we need to learn how to do it, and that is why we are enrolled in Adversity University. We just talked about looking unto Jesus, and then the very next verse tells us to "consider Him." It sounds to me like Jesus is pretty important! What does it mean to consider Jesus? It is not the same as the admonition to look to Him. The Greek word is analogizomai, which means to think over or ponder. It is the word from which we get our words "analyze" and "analysis." It means to think with the purpose of gaining a deep understanding of something or someone. Webster's Dictionary gives the meaning as "to view attentively." Considering Jesus means that we are paying attention to His person, His life, and His work.

This concept of considering is found in a number of places in the Bible. One of the most interesting is in Leviticus chapter 13. In those days, leprosy was a greatly feared disease. To prevent the disease from spreading, people who had leprosy were completely isolated from the rest of society. They could no longer live inside the camp with the rest of the children of Israel. Under the law, if a person thought they might have leprosy, they were to go to one of the priests for an inspection. Leviticus 13:13 says, "Then the priest shall consider..." This was not a cursory glance. The word means to thoroughly, meticulously, and personally evaluate. That is the way we are supposed to look at Jesus. God wants us to become meticulously acquainted with Jesus Christ—not just knowing the facts of His life, but to getting to know Him personally.

We must consider Jesus in order to successfully run our race. All of these concepts are linked together. First, we are told to run the race. Then, we are told to look to Jesus. Now, we are told to consider Him. Jesus Christ is the ultimate goal of our race. There are prizes to be won; rewards and crowns that we will receive for our service on Earth, but they are not the goal. God's plan and purpose for our race is that we will become like His Son. You need to have the goal clearly in mind when you start the race. American Kristen Armstrong won a cycling gold medal during the Beijing Olympics. Eight months before the games started, she went to Beijing and mapped out the course for the race. She entered it into a GPS system, and built a computer model to plan her strategy for each different section of the route. Knowing where she was headed and how she planned to get there gave her an advantage and helped her win the race.

We have to run. It is good to set goals, but wishing does not make anything happen. The old time farmers used to say, "The best place to pray for corn is at the end of the hoe handle." We have to run the race, and we need to look to Jesus while we run. We also must consider Jesus while we run. When we are running, it is imperative that we pattern our lives after the One who lived and ran the perfect race. All of these verbs—run, look, and consider—are continuous action verbs. It is consistent, repeated, ongoing action rather than a one-time thing. So, along the way, as we run, we need to be considering, "How can I know Him better? How can I pattern my life after Him? How would He respond to this situation, to this mountain, to this valley, or to this challenge that I am facing in my life?"

Cure for Discouragement

Considering Jesus Christ is God's cure for discouragement. Verse three says we consider Him "lest ye be wearied and faint in your minds." Can I let you in on a secret about the race? Runners quit in their minds, before they quit in their bodies. If He endured, if He kept running, if He refused to quit, then so can we, if we will consider why and how He remained faithful to the mission God had planned for His life. The race can cause us to become weary, so we need to be actively considering Jesus while we run.

The goal of being just like Jesus Christ is a wonderful goal, but it is a long-term goal. It is not something we are going to ever completely accomplish in this lifetime. What do I do about right know? What do I do when I am weary, I am tired, I want to give up, I want to quit, and I do not want to keep doing what God wants me to do? I know so many people who were once active runners, who fainted in their minds, and then stopped running. We need to know how to respond today. Notice what verse three says, we faint when we are weary. That is the contributing factor that makes us vulnerable to failure. Paul warned, "And let us not be weary in well doing: for in due season we shall reap, if we faint not." (Galatians 6:9)

Doing good, running well, and helping others can be discouraging. Sometimes we are tempted to say, "I have done my part, it is time for someone else to take over." We get weary serving the Lord. If we allow our weariness to take over, we faint. And Paul said that if we faint, we will not reap the rewards for our work. So, how can we keep from fainting? Consider Jesus! Think about Him. Evaluate Him. Analyze Him. Immerse yourself in the Bible and examine Him closely and attentively, like a doctor would search for an illness. Jesus is the example and pattern for us as we run the race. When He was tired, what did He do? The Bible tells us in John chapter 4.

Follow His Example

Then cometh he to a city of Samaria, which is called Sychar, near to the parcel of ground that Jacob gave to his son Joseph. Now Jacob's well was there. Jesus therefore, being wearied with his journey, sat thus on the well: and it was about the sixth hour (noon). (John 4:5-6)

While Jesus was resting, a woman came to draw water. Jesus talked to her and told her that He was the Living Water. She left her water pot at the well and ran into town to tell everyone that she had met the Messiah. What did Jesus do when He was tired? He ministered to someone in need! He did not take a break from teaching Sunday School or working on a bus route. He did not stay home from church because He was too tired to get up. He did not tell the pastor He was going to take a few weeks off from visitation. He ministered. When the disciples came back with food and encouraged Him to eat to renew His strength, He was already refreshed. He said, "My meat is to do the will of him that sent me, and to finish his work." (John 4:34) When you are tired, consider Jesus, and run your race the same way He ran His race.

When Christians get weary and drop out of the race, it does not just impact their lives; it affects everyone within their sphere of influence. It impacts the people they should be helping. What is the solution? Jesus hungered and thirsted to do God's will. When you get to the place where you "hunger and thirst after righteousness, for [you] shall be filled." (Matthew 5:6) When we are baby Christians, we hunger and thirst for the things He can do for us and give us. But, as we mature, we hunger and thirst for Him. He gives us the sustenance, the strength, and the courage to keep on keeping on. I cannot emphasize this too much—we do not need a kick in the seat of the pants, or a "pick me up" to get through another day. There is something more essential than that; we need to consider Jesus. He is the answer. He is the solution to our discouragement.

Investment of Time

So, knowing how important considering Jesus is, how do we do it? In a word, time. To think, evaluate, analyze, and examine something attentively and in depth requires and investment of time. Many times I have heard people say, "I don't have time." But, we all have the same amount of time; the problem is how we choose to prioritize and spend our time. Jesus must be our top priority. You can run for a while on the energy of an inspiring sermon. You can keep going for a while from rewards and pats on the back. But, if you depend on that, sooner or later it is not going to be there, and then what will you do? Paul put it this way:

But what things were gain to me, those I counted loss for Christ. Yea doubtless, and I count all things but loss for the excellency of the knowledge of Christ Jesus my Lord: for whom I have suffered the loss of all things things, and do count them but dung, that I may win Christ, And be found in him, not having mine own righteousness, which is of the law, but that which is through the faith of Christ, the righteousness which is of God by faith: That I may know him, and the power of his resurrection, and the fellowship of his sufferings, being made conformable unto his death. (Philippians 3:7-10)

If we are going to consider Christ—to make a scientific, in-depth study of Him—we are going to have to carve out the time to spend on it. We are going to have to set aside other distractions. There are always going to be things to compete for our time and attention. There are always going to be other things we could do. But, there is nothing more important than focusing on Jesus. What have you learned about Jesus this week? What have you learned in the last month? He is inexhaustible; there is no way we can ever learn all there is to know. The point of considering Jesus is not finding out more about Him; it is getting to know Him through studying the Scriptures in cooperation with the Spirit of God.

Become a Serious Student

It takes time, and it takes the Word. I hear a lot of preaching. But, much of it is shameful. I hear some people refer to all kinds of books and quote other preachers, but they hardly ever mention the Bible. I hear preachers read the text, and then they launch into their ideas and never mention the Bible again. We need to be serious students of Jesus Christ, and no one becomes a serious student of Jesus without first becoming a serious student of the Bible. It is the Jesus book. Get yourself some study tools like a Bible dictionary, a Webster's (1828) Dictionary and a good concordance like Strong's Concordance. Nothing else can substitute for getting alone with God in His book. Invest the time in listening and studying His Word while letting the Spirit of God teach you. That will keep you running the race even if everyone around you gets weary and drops out.

Hast thou not known? hast thou not heard, that the everlasting God, the Lord, the Creator of the ends of the earth, fainteth not, neither is weary? there is no searching of his understanding. He giveth power to the faint; and to them that have no might he increaseth strength. Even the youths shall faint and be weary, and the young men shall utterly fall: But they that wait upon the Lord shall renew their strength; they shall mount up with wings as eagles; they shall run, and not be weary; and they shall walk, and not faint. (Isaiah 40:28-31)

This is so encouraging. I know you may be reading this saying, "I have run out of strength. I'm weary. I can't keep going. I can't endure." Trying harder is not going to keep you going. Your best efforts in your own strength will utterly fail. But, if you wait on the Lord, your strength will be renewed. There are several Hebrew words for wait. The one used here comes from a Hebrew root word that means to bind together, as two strands are twisted together to make a rope. When Isaiah talked about waiting on the Lord, he was talking about being closely entwined with Him. That is the secret to having our strength renewed. That is the key to keeping on in the race and finishing well. Tie yourself to Jesus and consider Him, and He will carry you.

No matter who you are or what you do, you will get tired. It is not enough to commit to keep running. It is not enough just to look to Jesus. You will only overcome and keep running if you take the time to consider Him. Every time you face adversity, every time you face an obstacle, every time you have a problem, tie yourself to Jesus and wait on Him. He will renew your strength. Then, like Paul, you will be able to say, "I have fought a good fight, I have finished my course, I have kept the faith." (II Timothy 4:7)

7. When People Do Not Make Sense

"Wherefore seeing we also are compassed about with so great a cloud of witnesses, let us lay aside every weight and the sin which doth so easily beset us, and let us run with patience the race that is set before us. Looking unto Jesus the author and finisher of our faith, who for the joy that was set before Him endured the cross, despising the shame and is set down at the right hand at the throne of God. For consider him that endured such contradiction of sinners against himself, lest ye be wearied and faint in your mind." —Hebrews 12:1-3

Consider His Endurance

We see in this passage that Christ endured the cross, and we know that He ran the race, finished His course, and kept the faith. But, what does it mean to say that He endured such contradiction of sinners against Himself? Why did this occur in the life of Christ, Who is absolutely, completely, totally perfect? For what purpose did it occur? The word contradiction, if you divide it into two parts, you get *contra* (meaning against) and *diction* (meaning words.) Webster's Dictionary defines it this way: contradiction, an assertion of the contrary to what has been said or affirmed; a denial of a truth; or a statement or assertion of a contrary declaration.

The Greek word that is used here gives us further insight into the meaning of contradiction. It is the compound word *antilogia*, with *anti* meaning against, and *logia* meaning words. It is specifically using words or saying things that contradict or go contrary to what has been said. When the Lord lived on planet Earth, the Bible says He endured sinners contradicting themselves against Him. Now, this matter of contradiction is kind of like salsa; it can be mild, it can be medium, or it can be hot. I want us to do what this verse says and consider His endurance. Let me first give you an example of mild contradiction.

Mild Contradictions – Learn to Give Slack

"Now his parents went to Jerusalem every year at the feast of the Passover. And when he was twelve years old, they went up to Jerusalem after the custom of the feast. And when they had fulfilled the days, as they returned, the child Jesus tarried behind in Jerusalem; and Joseph and his mother knew not of it." (Luke 2:41-43)

Jesus experienced the contradiction of sinners within his own family. Despite what the Catholic church says, though Mary was a wonderful, godly woman, she was still a sinner who needed a Savior. Jewish people traveled to Jerusalem for three feasts, one of them being Passover. They would travel in groups for protection against thieves and bandits. After the feast was over, Joseph and Mary left for home, thinking that Jesus was in the group. I can imagine the scene as Mary and Joseph went through the camp, asking everyone if they had seen Jesus. I am sure, the longer they looked without finding Him, the more the panic grew and grew.

Finally, they realized that He was not there and decided to go back to Jerusalem. They were a day's journey from Jerusalem, so it took them another day to get back. Then, the Bible says they searched for him for three days. (Luke 2:46) By the time they found Jesus, Mary's twelve-year-old son had been missing for five days. It is important to understand the circumstances, because often when people are contradictory in what they say or what they do, there are extenuating circumstances. As a result of stress, fatigue, illness, or frustration, people say and do things that are completely out of character.

When they finally found Jesus after five days of worry and fear, Mary and Joseph were upset. In verse 48, we read, *"And when they saw him, they were amazed."* When we think of amazed, we usually picture something beautiful or stunning, but that is not the word that is used here. They were flabbergasted. The word used carries the meaning of being afflicted with calamity. I imagine Mary's eyes were red from crying. She said, *"Son, why hast thou thus dealt with us? behold, thy father and I have sought thee sorrowing."* Now, Jesus was all God. He was in a twelve-year-old body, but He was still completely God. He could have lectured Mary about His Divine purpose and nature and infallibility. Instead, He simply said, *"wist [know] ye not that I must be about my Father's business?"* (Luke 2:49) What a mild response. He corrected her erroneous statement that implied Joseph was His father, but his reaction showed no arrogance or cockiness.

If you even could call that a rebuke, then it is certainly very mild. The Bible tells us that He went home with His parents and was in subjection to them. (Luke 2:51) Jesus was contradicted by His mother, but He was patient with her. Give slack to good people. If we are not careful, we will allow an unusual reaction from someone to stick in our craw and irritate us and cause us to react. Hebrews 12 says that if we are not careful, the contradiction of sinners can cause us to be wearied and even faint—lose heart and give up. Even mild contradictions can cause us to blow things out of proportion and ruin good relationships. Sometimes, however, the contradictions are more serious. Look with me at John 7.

Medium Contradictions – Do Not React

After these things Jesus walked in Galilee: for he would not walk in Jewry, because the Jews sought to kill him. Now the Jews' feast of tabernacles was at hand. His brethren therefore said unto him, Depart hence, and go into Judaea, that thy disciples also may see the works that thou doest. For there is no man that doeth any thing in secret, and he himself seeketh to be known openly. If thou do these things, shew thyself to the world. For neither did his brethren believe in him. (John 7:1-5)

Here, again, we see Jesus enduring contradiction from His family. His brothers, the other children of Mary and Joseph, had grown up with Jesus, but they did not believe in Him. You would think that if anyone would have believed, it would be those who knew Him best; but as you saw in the title of this chapter, people often do not make sense. In fact, his brothers challenged Jesus to risk His life and go where people were trying to kill Him.

Yet, we never see Jesus react, even when those who should have believed in Him the most did not. He could have said, "You want to see proof that I'm the Son of God? Let Me see what I can do to you!" He could have parked them thirty feet up in the air. He could have walked through the wall of their house. He could have done all sorts of things. But Jesus was non-reactive. We want to react. We want to defend ourselves. The more severe the contradiction is, the greater our need to respond seems to be. But we simply never find Jesus defending Himself. That was even true with the most severe contradictions. Look at Mark 3.

Severe Contradictions – Respond with Endurance

And the multitude cometh together again, so that they could not so much as eat bread. And when his friends heard of it, they went out to lay hold on him: for they said, He is beside himself. And the scribes which came down from Jerusalem said, He hath Beelzebub, and by the prince of the devils casteth he out devils. (Mark 3:20-22)

Jesus had just finished casting out a demon who declared that He was the Son of God. What did His friends say? "That Jesus is plumb crazy. He's going out of his mind!" You would think that someone who was your friend, someone you grew up with and played with, someone you went to school with would stand by you. Not Jesus' friends. They tried to have Him committed! That is a contradiction of sinners.

He never reacted. He did not rebuke His friends. He suffered that contradiction, that adversity, without fainting or failing. Jesus endured, always responding appropriately to the situation whether it was mild, medium, or hot. The contradiction of sinners is more than just conversation; it goes to the very heart of our commitments. The reality of life and people is that they do not make sense. They make commitments and then do not keep them. We see this dramatically illustrated in Matthew 21 with the story of Jesus' triumphal entry into Jerusalem.

And a very great multitude spread their garments in the way; others cut down branches from the trees, and strawed them in the way. And the multitudes that went before, and that followed, cried, saying, Hosanna to the Son of David: Blessed is he that cometh in the name of the Lord; Hosanna in the highest. (Matthew 21:8-9)

The people gave Jesus a royal welcome to the city of Jerusalem. You could not possibly get a better response than He received. The people were celebrating and rejoicing. They were ready to proclaim Him as the King. That happened on what we call Palm Sunday. Now, look at Matthew 27 and see what happened to the people that same week:

But the chief priests and elders persuaded the multitude that they should ask Barabbas, and destroy Jesus. The governor answered and said unto them, Whether of the twain will ye that I release unto you? They said, Barabbas. Pilate saith unto them, What shall I do then with Jesus which is called Christ? They all say unto him, Let him be crucified. And the governor said, Why, what evil hath he done? But they cried out the more, saying, Let him be crucified. (Matthew 27:20-23)

You know that the multitude of Matthew 27 had to include some of the same people who were part of the multitude of Matthew 21. What a dichotomy. What a contradiction. One day, they were saying, "Welcome Jesus, King of the Jews. We're so excited that You're here." Then, a few days later, they said, "Release unto us Barabbas. Take this Jesus and crucify Him. Crucify Him!" What happened? Four-day loyalty? Four-day commitment? People do not make sense. That is a real contradiction.

Contradiction of Commitment

The chief priests and elders persuaded the people to change their minds. There are going to be people who will try to persuade you to compromise on the commitments that you have made to Jesus Christ. That is the reality of our world. You may face this pressure even from leaders and those who are respected in the community. What will you do in the day of adversity? How will you endure the contradiction of sinners?

Sometimes, the contradiction comes from those who are the closest to us in the world. Sometimes, it is very personal. In Matthew 16 Jesus asked, *"Whom do men say that I the Son of man am?"* (Matthew 16:13) Then, Jesus asked who the disciples thought He was. Peter responded, *"Thou art the Christ, the Son of the living God."* (Matthew 16:16) Yet, just a few verses later, everything changes. Jesus began to explain to the disciples that He must be crucified and rise again from the dead. Matthew 16:22 says, *"Peter took him."* That means, he literally grabbed Jesus with his hands and pulled Him to himself. Today, we would say Peter 'got in His face.' *"This shall not be!"* Peter said. That is a contradiction.

How could Peter go from speaking directly by the gift of God to speaking with the voice of the Devil to contradict what he had just said? How does that happen? There is a real Devil in the world who is working nonstop to influence people to do wrong. Peter would later write, *"Be sober, be vigilant; because your adversary the devil, as a roaring lion, walketh about, seeking whom he may devour."* (I Peter 5:8) I wonder if when the Holy Spirit gave him those words, Peter thought about that day when Jesus rebuked him—that day when the Devil influenced him to contradict his commitment to Jesus.

Offense Shows Lack of Faith

Notice what Jesus did. He did rebuke Peter, sharply. *"Get thee behind me, Satan"* is a pretty strong statement. (The closer people were to Jesus, the more dynamic He was in His interactions with them.) But, through all of these contradictions, Jesus never got defensive. He was never offended by the words or actions of others. Understanding the concept of offense is crucial to learning how to endure contradictions.

Peter answered and said unto him, Though all men shall be offended because of thee, yet will I never be offended. Jesus said unto him, Verily I say unto thee, That this night, before the cock crow, thou shalt deny me thrice. Peter said unto him, though I should die with thee, yet will I not deny thee. Likewise, also said all the disciples. (Matthew 26:33-35)

Jesus identified why the disciples would contradict their commitment and forsake Him. It was not because they were afraid. It was not because they were discouraged. It was not because they lacked faith. That is not what Jesus said. He said they were going to be offended. This is where they add extra jalapeños, and the salsa gets hot. These men had spent three years and six months under the personal training of Jesus Christ, the Son of God. They were coming to the crisis hour of His life and theirs, and Jesus said they would be offended.

The word offended means scandalized. These men, when they saw Jesus led away, obviously to be crucified, concluded that Jesus was contradicting Himself. Read these words very carefully; this is why good people give up and go bad. They wrongly perceive that God is not being true to His commitment. They get offended; and as a result of being offended, they break their commitments. That is exactly what the disciples did. The problem was that they did not see the big picture—and neither do you. You look at what is happening and say, "Well, God, if You are really fair, why would You do this to me? You disappoint me. You're letting me down." God is bigger than you think He is. He has a plan for your life, and you must never forget that truth.

Overcome the Adversity of Contradiction

All through His life, Jesus endured the contradiction of sinners. We have looked at contradictions from His parents, His brothers, His friends, and His disciples. It started out when he was a child. It was mild. Then, it got more intense. People broke not only their word, contradicting what they said, but they also broke their commitments. Why did Jesus not get offended and give up? He believed in God's plan. Even when things were tough, He trusted the Father completely.

When the people around you, who love you, contradict themselves and hurt you, it is a temptation. You are tempted to say, "I'm angry.

I did my best. Look how they repaid me! Listen to them contradict what they know and what they said. He said he'd love me forever. She promised she'd do this or stop doing that. I remember the commitments they made. How dare they say those things to me now so blatantly, and so boldly?"

People do not make sense. So, what are you going to do about it? The Bible says Jesus endured it. So must we endure. He always responded appropriately and unselfishly. When the people who had cried out for Him to be king contradicted that and said, "Crucify him," He picked up the cross and allowed Himself to be crucified. When the disciples were offended and forsook Him, He kept loving them. When Peter denied Him, Jesus restored him to fellowship. That is what God wants us to do. If we endure contradiction, then we may get weary, but we will not faint. Those who endure instead of being offended and those who overcome the adversity of contradiction, are the ones who receive the joy that is prepared for them by the Father.

8. The Ultimate Freedom Fighters

"Looking unto Jesus the author and finisher of our faith; who for the joy that was set before him endured the cross, despising the shame, and is set down at the right hand of the throne of God. For consider him that endured such contradiction of sinners against himself, lest ye be wearied and faint in your minds. Ye have not yet resisted unto blood, striving against sin." —Hebrews 12:2-4

We are Soldiers

We hear a lot today about freedom fighters. Sometimes, it refers to people who are fighting against a brutal and repressive government. Sometimes, the term is inappropriately used for terrorists who trying to kill brave American soldiers around the world. But, the ultimate freedom fighters are found in the spiritual realm. I am talking about those who, for the cause of Christ, resist unto blood, striving against sin. To properly understand this expression, we need to grasp a word picture that God wants us to visualize. This is a picture of a soldier. The words that are given to us here in verse 4—resisting, striving, and bleeding—are all words of war. This is not a picture of diplomacy; this is a picture of an all-out conflict.

I want you to picture the concept being taught here. The Bible often compares the Christian life to the life of a soldier. At the end of his life, Paul would say, "I have fought a good fight." (II Timothy 4:7) He wrote to Timothy, "Fight the good fight." (I Timothy 6:12) The Bible exhorts us to be good soldiers of Jesus Christ. (II Timothy 2:3) We are to live our lives in such a way unencumbered by the things of this world, that we may please Him who has called us to be a soldier. The reality of the Christian life is that it is a battlefield; it is a war. What the author of Hebrews is saying here is that we have to be willing to fight, even to the point of shedding blood.

The Bible uses the word striving to describe the contention with the adversary that we endure in this battle. It is the Greek word antagonizomai; the root word from which we get our word agony. Surely it is an agonizing battle against sin that we face. Verse three tells us to consider Jesus. Let's look at Him resisting sin. Even before He went to the cross, He sweat great drops of blood as He prayed that if it were possible, the cup could pass from Him. (Luke 22:41-44) The physical suffering He endured from the crucifixion is almost unimaginable. He was beaten, scourged with a cat of nine tails. Isaiah said His visage would be more marred than any other man. (Isaiah 52:14) And the physical suffering, resisting unto blood, was nothing compared to the emotional and ethical pain Jesus suffered as He took our sins on the cross and was separated from the Father.

Faithful unto Death

Many of the heroes of the faith that we saw in chapter 11 resisted unto blood. Some of them, like Daniel and the three Hebrew children, were delivered. But, many others were not. They courageously suffered for their faith, even unto blood.

Women received their dead raised to life again: and others were tortured, not accepting deliverance; that they might obtain a better resurrection: And others had trial of cruel mockings and scourgings, yea, moreover of bonds and imprisonment: They were stoned, they were sawn asunder, were tempted, were slain with the sword: they wandered about in sheepskins and goatskins; being destitute, afflicted, tormented. (Hebrews 11:35-37)

The word used here for torture is tympanum, the word from which we get timpani. They would take the person who was to be punished and tie them to a wheel, just as the skin is stretched over a drum. Then, they would beat the person, breaking the skin and even the bones. It was not uncommon for people to die from the beating they received. Yet, despite facing this torture, these heroes refused deliverance. They resisted unto blood.

Some were "sawn asunder." The Roman Law of Twelve Tables established this method of execution. The condemned person would be encased in a tight wooden box, and then the box would be cut in half with the person inside. Most of the time, they would cut the person in half across the middle; but if the crime was particularly heinous, they would cut the person from head to foot. What an awful way to die! Tradition tells us that the prophet Isaiah was martyred by being cut in half. They were truly faithful until death.

Two times in my life I have visited death row in a prison. Last year, I went to Angola Prison in Louisiana. At that time, there were 160 men on Death Row, awaiting execution. It was a sobering experience. They took us into the room where the executions are carried out. I am in favor of capital punishment, because the Bible supports it. I believe it is a deterrent to crime when properly applied. But, to see it firsthand brings home the seriousness of what it really means. The heroes of the faith and our Savior did not yield when they faced adversity—they resisted even unto blood.

The question for us today is whether we are willing to follow their admonition and example. I confess to you that I am not sure I would have the grace to do that. I hope I never have to face that choice. Because we live in America, we are largely insulated from serious persecution. However, do not be so naive as to think that it could not happen here. It has happened before. Patrick Henry, one of the heroes of the American Revolution, is best known to us for saying, "Give me liberty or give me death." But, he was famous in colonial Virginia as a lawyer who defended Baptist preachers who were put in jail for preaching without taking a license from the state. If our country continues on the path that we are rushing down away from God, we could go back to a time of persecution. The peace and tranquility that we have enjoyed for so many years in our country is at risk today.

Enemy of Sin

Can you picture and visualize the enemy? We often think of our war against Satan. And certainly, Satan is our enemy. But, he is not the subject of Hebrews 12:4. The enemy we must resist is sin. This passage is not talking about striving against a person or group of people. The cause that is set before us is reaching the world with the Gospel. The enemy is sin. Anything that hinders us from fulfilling the calling of God, to run the race that is set before us, to know Christ and to make him known is sin. The reason we resist sin is for the sake of the cause.

Philippians 3:14 uses the same word when Paul said, "I press toward the mark for the prize of the high calling of God in Christ Jesus." When we got saved, God gave us a higher calling—to go into all the world and preach the Gospel. We are to bring men to Christ, bring them to baptism in a local New Testament Church, and then helping to disciple them to spiritual maturity. That calling is given to each and every one of us just as assuredly as it was given to Peter and Paul and the other apostles.

Sadly, I did not recognize this calling until I had been saved for ten years. But, when I was fifteen or sixteen years of age, I began to see and to sense that God had a bigger purpose for my life than simply saving me from the penalty of sin and the power of sin. He had a church for me to pastor and people for me to win to Him. When we recognize the calling and purpose God has for us, it puts the matter of resisting sin unto blood in a whole new light. Sin is the enemy. Sin is the enemy of faith. Sin is the enemy of soul winning. Therefore, it must be removed. We were not sent into the world simply to fight sin; we are also fighting for the freedom of those who are in bondage to sin. How can we effectively see God use us to set people free from the bondage of sin if we are in bondage to sin ourselves?

My Battle

I want you to not only see the concept of resisting that is given to us, but I want you to personalize the criticism. The writer said, "Ye have not yet resisted unto blood striving against sin." What an indictment. We have to recognize that there is a constant struggle, a war that must be waged against sin. I must personalize it for myself if I am going to win that battle. No one else can do that for me. By the grace of God, I must be willing to resist anything that will keep me back or hinder me or cause me to miss the mark. What is it that causes a Christian to lose his or her burden for winning the lost? What is it that blinds us to the needs of the world? It is our sin. Instead of living our lives as if everything revolves around getting ahead, we must see that there is a much bigger purpose here for our lives.

But call to remembrance the former days, in which, after ye were illuminated, ye endured a great fight of afflictions; Partly, whilst ye were made a gazingstock both by reproaches and afflictions; and partly, whilst ye became companions of them that were so used. For ye had compassion of me in my bonds, and took joyfully the spoiling of your goods, knowing in yourselves that ye have in heaven a better and an enduring substance. Cast not away therefore your confidence, which hath great recompense of reward. (Hebrews 10:32-35)

These believers to whom Hebrews was written had wonderful testimonies. It is surprising to see them criticized for not resisting sin. These were men and women who had begun with Christ with great zeal and great desire to be sacrificial. Yet, somewhere along the way, perhaps because of the intensity of the struggle, or perhaps due to the allurements of the world around them, they reached a point of great danger. They were about to cast away their confidence in the Lord. They wanted to fit in. They did not want to be odd. They had started well, but they were not resisting unto blood. The cost of living for God is very high.

We enjoy the testimonies of the men and women who laid the foundations for us in the first century of Christianity. We admire them. Stephen was stoned to death. Matthew was slain in Ethiopia. Mark was dragged through the streets until he was dead. Luke was hanged. Peter and Simeon were crucified. Andrew was tied to a cross. James was beheaded. Philip was crucified and stoned. Bartholomew was flayed alive. Thomas was pierced with lances. James the Less was thrown from the Temple and beaten to death. Jude was shot with arrows. Matthias was stoned to death. And Paul was beheaded. The second century church father Tertullian said, "The blood of the martyrs is the seed of the church."

Pursue the Cause

We have been blessed with the heritage of faith of those who have come before. Will we fail the test? Will we allow other responsibilities and obligations to take the place of God's higher calling? The will of God is for us to know Christ and make Him known. That is the reason you and I are still here. We must strive against sin, even to blood, for the sake of those who came before, and so we can reach the great cause. And to reach the prize, we must pursue the cause.

It is no coincidence that Hebrews 12:2 calls Jesus the "finisher of our faith." The danger is that we can get off course and not finish the race if we lose our focus on the cause. I recently heard a politician say, "It's time to stop spending money on a war in another part of the world and spend that money on social programs and meeting the needs of our American citizens that are undergoing such severe privation because of the economic stress." That is the statement of someone who has lost sight of the purpose of the war. When we lose sight of the purpose, we lose our vision for it and our willingness to resist unto blood. We become willing to compromise anything. Our purpose as believers is not simply resisting being dissuaded by sin; our goal is to know Christ and to make Him known.

The pursuit of that goal makes it imperative that we fight anything that will hinder us from fulfilling that higher calling God has given to us. But, never forget that fighting against sin is simply a means to an end. Sometimes, we think the reason why the devil tries to get us off track is so that he can ruin our lives. That is not it at all. The reason the devil sends adversity to get us off track and involved in sin is so he can keep us from the cause. He sees what you can be used of God to accomplish and wants to hinder that calling. When the main thing remains your goal, you can effectively deal with sin. The great tragedy of sin is that it hinders us from doing what God has called us to do.

I told you earlier that when I was sixteen years of age, I began catching a vision and glimpse of a higher calling from God for my life. I had two best friends when I was a teenager. Depending on who you asked, Dan, Dave, and I were either the Three Musketeers or the Three

Stooges. We went to church together, but we each went to a different high school. God was working in each of our lives, and we all surrendered to do His will. We learned how to be soul winners. I started preaching in the county jail. I had the same struggles ever sixteen-year-old boy has to stay pure and live right. But, when I caught a vision of the higher calling of God, it changed my attitude towards the battle.

We made a pact that we would serve Christ and hold each other accountable. All three of us had girlfriends. We were not allowed to date in high school. (I don't believe high school is a time for boys and girls to date.) But, each of us had a girl we liked—I am married to that girl today! The girl Dave liked was named Beth. Though she was a Christian, she was not really dedicated to the Lord. Dave's parents said, "Beth's not a dedicated Christian, and you've dedicated your life to the cause." Dave broke up with Beth. Dan also had a girlfriend. Just like Dave's girlfriend, she was a Christian, but she was not dedicated. Dan's parents told him the same thing Dave's parents had.

But, unlike Dave, Dan resisted. Dave and I tried to talk to him and warn him about what we saw. He stopped going soul winning. When we got together, he wanted to talk about her instead of talking about the Bible. He downplayed our concerns and said, "Oh man, it'll be all right." If you can believe it, we sang together in a trio. One Sunday night, we were singing in church. In the middle of a song about serving Christ, Dan started weeping uncontrollably. He walked off the stage, and the song ended. We sat next to him, and with tears streaming down his face, Dan told us that his girlfriend was pregnant. Can I tell you what happened? That young man lost sight of the cause. And, when you lose sight of the cause, you become more vulnerable to sin. You will find yourself unwilling to resist sin unto blood, striving against it.

Dave is with the Lord now; but all of his life, he was a faithful, godly man. Of all the men that I have known, he was one of the top two or three men in my life that I admired the most. He was an incredible soldier of Jesus Christ. How different his life would have been if he had lost sight of the cause and succumbed to sin. As far as I know, Dan never got back into the cause. He did not resist unto blood, and the devil won a victory. But, that is not the greatest tragedy. Dan did not focus on the cause. It is not just about striving against sin; it is about focusing on the cause. When you do, you will be a real freedom fighter.

9. The Forgotten Exhortation

"And ye have forgotten the exhortation which speaketh unto you as unto children, My son, despise not thou the chastening of the Lord, nor faint when thou art rebuked of him: For whom the Lord loveth he chasteneth, and scourgeth every son whom he receiveth." —Hebrews 12:5-6

Purpose of Chastening

In order to successfully graduate from Adversity University and take our place with the extraordinary and exceptional men and women of faith, we have to run the race, look away from the world and to Jesus, and resist unto blood for the sake of the cause. But, here we see another exhortation that we must remember—the purpose of chastening. Proverbs 3:11-12 says it this way, *"My son, despise not the chastening of the Lord; neither be weary of his correction: For whom the Lord loveth he correcteth; even as a father the son in whom he delighteth."*

We know this truth, but many of us have forgotten it. This is why the author of Hebrews is giving us an educational passage. In fact, the meaning of the word *chastening* is to educate or to train. I took trigonometry and calculus in school; but I guarantee you, if you gave me a math test, once I got past addition, subtraction, multiplication, division, and maybe algebra, I would be lost. I was taught those concepts, but I have forgotten. We tend to forget what we do not use regularly. That is just as true of the Bible as it is of math. We are not talking about bad people—good, saved people forget the Bible if they do not use it regularly.

Notice that the Bible is not just a book from the past. Verse 5 says, *"the exhortation which speaketh"*—the verb is a present, active, continuous tense—*"unto you."* The Bible is alive. Hebrews 4:12 says, *"The word of God is quick."* Peter said, *"Being born again, not of corruptible seed, but of incorruptible, by the word of God, which liveth and abideth for ever."* (I Peter 1:23) The Bible is not just alive, it is also personal. It speaks directly and specifically to us. The words in Scripture are letters from God to you and me. That makes some people uncomfortable, which is why they stop reading and listening to the Word...and why they forget what it says. We take the Bible casually and forget its precepts, because we do not treat it as a living letter written personally to us.

I do not know how many times over the years someone has said to me, "Preacher, I'm sure glad you preached that sermon. Brother So-and-So sure needed to hear it!" It is easy to see how the Bible applies to others and think that it is written for them. But, God is speaking to your heart through its pages. I want to make sure that you understand what this passage has to say for your life.

God Speaks To Us as His Children

Now, when I say we are God's children, I am not talking about humanity in general. That relationship is only for those who are saved. I was born the first time as the son of Richard Kingsbury. Five years later, on a Sunday night in March, when I accepted Jesus Christ as my Savior, I was born as a son of the Heavenly Father. I have a personal, intimate relationship with Him. What an amazing concept that is! Jesus said, *"Are not two sparrows sold for a farthing? and one of them shall not fall on the ground without your Father."* (Matthew 10:29-30) If you ask me, sparrows are pretty worthless. The only thing I know they are good for is to keep car washes in business. But, every time a seemingly worthless bird dies, the Father knows it. If we forget that truth, then we are on our way to spiritual misery.

God Chastens Us as His Children

In this verse, we also see that **God chastens us as His children.** When we think of chastening, we usually think of corporal punishment. But what is being talked about here is an all-encompassing process as God educates and trains us to become mature believers who live by faith in Him. If we want the good report that comes from faith, then we have to endure the adversity that helps mature us as believers. God chastens us because we are His children, and He wants us to learn His ways. Remember that the purpose of chastening is our education.

By the way, if you have never experienced God's chastening, Hebrews 12 says that you should be worried about whether you are really part of His family or not. If you do not recognize His chastening, then you are missing the experience that is common to every child of God. He enrolled you in the University of Adversity on the day that you were saved, and He will keep you there until He calls you home.

God Rebukes Us as His Children

The Bible calls this whole program God's chastening. There are different parts of chastening—different classes in school. We also see here that **God rebukes us as His children.** When the word "rebuke" is used in the New Testament, it is with the idea of pointing out a problem. In Matthew 18:15, the same Greek word is translated "*tell him his fault.*"

You may hear your fault pointed out by a preacher or Sunday School teacher, or the Holy Spirit may bring conviction as you read a verse of Scripture. A rebuke is a verbal identification of an area in your life that is wrong. I have heard people say, "I don't want to go to that church; because when I go there, I feel bad." Why do they feel bad? It is because their loving Heavenly Father is rebuking them instead of allowing them to continue doing wrong. When you get into the Bible, or when you go to church and God speaks to you and rebukes you, that is not something to run away from; it is a wonderful blessing. Rebuke shows that you belong to Him, and that He loves you perfectly. Not only that, but He *knows* you.

When we work with our children as parents, we do not have perfect knowledge. We cannot know everything about them and exactly what they need. But, God knows everything about us. Everything that comes into your life—every blessing and every irritation—is put there because you are His child. We need to learn to listen for the still, small voice of the Spirit of God and respond to His internal conviction. He is telling us our faults, admonishing us, and reproving us for them. We should be grateful that He does.

God Loves Us as His Children

Next, we see that **God loves us as His children**. It is possible to chasten someone and not care a whit about them. But, that is not true of our Father in Heaven. He loves us with a love that is far more than simply emotional. His love is unselfish, sacrificial, and absolutely, completely committed to meeting our every need. That is the love we see demonstrated as Jesus hung on Calvary's cross. It is dangerous to forget God's love. When we are chastened, the devil whispers to us, "God doesn't like you very much, does He? Just look at the guy across the street. He's every bit as bad as you, but he gets away with it." Do not let chastening make you doubt God's love. It is proof that you are His child.

God does not necessarily bring chastening on the devil's children. I did not spank the neighbor's kids; I spanked mine. There were times I wanted to; but I didn't, because they did not have my name. Every day, moment by moment, God is looking at your life and bringing circumstances to pass to chasten, educate, train, and mature you into a person of extraordinary faith. I have heard people say, "I didn't have nearly as many problems before I got saved as I do now." That is because when they got saved, they were enrolled in God's University of Adversity.

What happens when you are in school and have to go to the principal's office? I have *heard* that there is correction. No, I know it, because I got chastened in junior high school. When you don't listen and don't listen, the chastening gets harder and harder. It gets progressively more painful until you respond. Why? It is because God loves you. A parent who does not discipline their child does not really love them. Proverbs 13:24 says, *"He that spareth his rod hateth his son: but he that loveth him chasteneth him betimes (early)."* God keeps correcting until we listen. When you have been through that process enough times, and you finally repent of your wicked sin and confess and forsake it, then you will find His mercy. We cannot forget this exhortation.

God Scourges Us as His Children

Notice then that **God scourges us as His children**. This is far beyond rebuke. Rebuke is at the verbal level. Scourging is painful, physical punishment. In fact, this word is exactly the same word for the torture Jesus endured at the hands of the Roman soldiers where they whipped Him until the flesh was torn from His back. If we do not listen when God talks, He will scourge us. God takes our spiritual development seriously. He will not let His children continue to ignore His voice.

Do you know when God is scourging you? Or, do you chalk it up to bad luck or blame someone else for what is going wrong in your life? God scourges you. Why? It is because He loves you. When you suffer adversity in life, it is not always because you have sinned. That is the mistake Job's friends made; they assumed Job's suffering was caused by secret sins. We live in a fallen world; and sometimes, bad things do happen to good people. But, when things go wrong, examine your life, and see if God is trying to use that pain to scourge you to heed and follow Him.

God Receives Us as His Children

In this passage, we also see that **God receives us as His children.** The word *receive* means to accept or be near. This is so important to remember. After the chastening, the rebuke, and the scourging, when we repent and forsake our sin, He takes us back. We see this illustrated so beautifully in the parable of the Prodigal Son. As soon as the boy was ready to come home, the father accepted him with open arms. He did not hold the past against him; he did not reprove him for wasting his substance. Instead, he threw a party to celebrate the return. That is how God treats His children. When the goal has been accomplished, there is a complete restoration and acceptance.

I know people who have not been blessed with that kind of relationship here on earth. They have been rejected and pushed away by their parents. If that is true for you, I have got some good news. It will never be that way with your Father in Heaven. On the basis of the unchanging and unfailing Word of God, I guarantee you that when you return to Him, He will receive you. The prophet Isaiah said, *"Let the wicked forsake his way, and the unrighteous man his thoughts: and let him return unto the Lord, and he will have mercy upon him; and to our God, for he will abundantly pardon."* (Isaiah 55:7)

This is serious business. Let me call your attention to the warning Paul gave to the church at Corinth regarding the way they were celebrating the Lord's Supper.

Wherefore whosoever shall eat this bread, and drink this cup of the Lord, unworthily, shall be guilty of the body and blood of the Lord. But let a man examine himself, and so let him eat of that bread, and drink of that cup. For he that eateth and drinketh unworthily, eateth and drinketh damnation to himself, not discerning the Lord's body. For this cause many are weak and sickly among you, and many sleep. For if we would judge ourselves, we should not be judged. (I Corinthians 11:27-31)

Damnation! What a word. Now, we know this is not talking about being condemned to hell, because it is written to saved people. It means judgment and carries the idea of being ruined. If you do not respond with repentance, you are bringing great trouble into your life. Many are weak and sick, and many sleep. When you do not heed God's chastening, your will and strength to do right are diminished. Disobedience robs us of the strength and the stamina that we need to endure as well as to do the will of God, to obtain a good report, to grow and develop spiritually, and to pass the courses in the University of Adversity. If we still refuse to respond, we become spiritually ill. There are many Christians who have fallen asleep spiritually speaking. It is a great tragedy.

However, I do not think this passage is simply talking about spiritual weakness and sickness. If we refuse to respond when we are corrected, God will bring weakness, sickness, and even premature death to us. God will work with you, work with you, work with you, and work with you, trying to bring you to the point of repentance. But, there comes a time when He says, "I'm just going to leave you to go your own direction. You do not want to listen to Me, so I'm not going to speak to you anymore." Proverbs 29:1 says, *"He, that being often reproved hardeneth his neck, shall suddenly be destroyed, and that without remedy."* This is serious business. This forgotten exhortation is so important for us in our walk with the Lord. If there is anything that God has been talking to you about that you need to change by His grace, trust Him, and change it.

10. Responding to God's Chastening

"And ye have forgotten the exhortation which speaketh unto you as unto children. My son, despise not thou the chastening of the Lord, nor faint when thou art rebuked of him: For whom the Lord loveth he chasteneth, and scourgeth every son whom he receiveth." —Hebrews 12:5-6

Response Determines Future

We talked in the last chapter about what we need to remember when we face chastening from the Lord. Now let's look at how we respond to that chastening. When God chastens, corrects, rebukes, chastises, and scourges us, our response determines our future. I remember it like it was yesterday. I was twelve years old, and it was Sunday. In my house, in 1965, the Lord's Day was a day of rest. There was no playing outside allowed. We could not watch television. After church, Mom would fix a big meal, and we would all sit down and eat together.

The one thing we were allowed to do on Sunday afternoons was listen to music. Mom and Dad had a big box stereo and a stack of record albums. They had Bill Pierce and Dick Anthony, the White Sisters, Ethel Waters, and the good music of the era. On this particular Sunday, Danny and Mike came over and asked if I could come out and play with them. I looked at my pals and said casually, "Guys, you know I can't come outside. It's Sunday and my old man won't…." I knew immediately. I did not see him, but I knew that he was standing right behind me. I was watching Danny and Mike. Their eyes got as big as silver dollars, their lips began to quiver, and they began to back up. In that moment, I made the decision that would determine my immediate future. In that split second, I thought, "I'm 12; he's 40. I can outrun him." I made it past the Parker's house. I made it past the Hike's house. But, I did not make it past the Green's house. There was a bloody mess in the front yard of Mr. & Mrs. Green's home that afternoon. They were looking out the windows to see what the noise was all about. Today, parents would probably call 9-1-1. But, back in those days they were cheering. "Get him, Dick, get him!" And he did! What happened that day? I made a very foolish choice in how I responded to Dad's correction. The good news is that I was able to sit down again by the time I started ninth grade!

This passage from Hebrews tells us that there are two foolish responses to God's chastening. If you choose either of these responses, you are determining your destiny. You are guaranteeing yourself more trouble than you had to start with in the first place. These two choices are different; in fact, they almost stand in opposition to each other. But, they are both wrong responses.

Despising His Chastening

Every child of God receives chastening from Him. We need it. We are not perfect. So God chastens, corrects, rebukes, and sometimes even scourges us. What happens next depends on how we respond. The first response we see is despising His chastening. The word "despise" means "to think very little of." The first time it is used in the Bible is in the story of the feeding of the five thousand. Jesus asked Andrew what they had to feed them with, and he said, "two small fishes." (John 6:9) It is the same root word. We despise God's chastening when we realize that

He is speaking to us and working in our lives, but we do not think it is important for us to pay attention. People who despise God's chastening eventually become oblivious to it. They choose to ignore His warnings and ignore His chastening. That is a terrible decision to make.

Do you realize how wonderful, gracious, and kind it is of God to chasten you, to correct you when you go astray, rebuke you when you are wrong, and to scourge you if need be? What if instead, He simply destroyed us the moment we stepped out of line? Instead, He lovingly offers us reminders to bring us to repentance. Despising the Lord's chastening begins with despising the Word of the Lord. If you and I have a proper respect for the Word of the Lord and what He says to us through His Word, then we will have little problem with this matter of despising the chastening of the Lord. The Bible calls us to a life that is beyond our own capabilities to ever accomplish. God does that, not to frustrate or to discourage us, but so that we will depend completely upon Him. Though it is impossible for us to live the Christ-life ourselves, it is totally possible with Christ. (Philippians 4:13) He is honored and glorified when we exercise Biblical faith.

Despise Authority – Despise the Lord

When God chastens, corrects, and rebukes us and we despise it, what we are revealing is that we think very little of His Word. But, that is not the end of the process. If we continue to despise His Word and His chastening, we will also begin to despise His preachers. When Jesus sent the seventy out two by two, He told them, "He that heareth you heareth me; and he that despiseth you despiseth me; and he that despiseth me despiseth him that sent me." (Luke 10:16) God has appointed and ordained people in your life to teach you and speak His Word. They speak on his behalf. If you ignore and despise them, then you are ignoring and despising Him. I have heard people say, "Well that's just my parents' opinion." Others may say, "The preacher thinks that, but I'm upset with him. I don't like what he said." If the preacher is giving you the Word of God, and you despise it, you are not really despising him. It is much worse than that.

Do you remember the story of Samuel in the Old Testament? Samuel spent his whole life preaching to the children of Israel and exalting God. Near the end of his life, the children of Israel came to him and said, "Listen, Samuel, we want a king." Samuel was discouraged by that. When he told the Lord about it, the Lord made a statement that encouraged Samuel, but profoundly rebuked the people. "Hearken unto the voice of the people and all that they say unto thee, for they have not rejected thee, but they have rejected me." (I Samuel 8:7) When we think little of the chastening, the correcting, the rebuking of God; it strikes at our relationship with God Himself. Rebellion against the authorities God has placed in your life is not simply rebellion against their rules and regulations or their guidance. It is rebellion and rejection against the Word and Person of God.

During my years in the ministry, I have counseled thousands of people who were being chastened. On only a handful of those occasions have I had someone come into my office and say, "Preacher, I'm not right with God. I've been in rebellion against God, and God is chastening me. I want help." Instead, they almost always blame someone else, complain that God isn't being fair to them, express their bitterness about what is happening, or gripe about how no one helps them. Why is it that so many people despise God's chastening? I think many people have gotten so oblivious to God in their lives that they think they can actually live contrary to His Word without experiencing His correction, His chastening and His chastisement. That is a dangerous place to be.

It is a guarantee that you are going to experience increased heartache, increased sorrow, increased pain, increased suffering, and increased chastening from the hand of God.

At the moment, when I determined that Dad heard what I said about him, I could have saved myself a memorable whipping with repentance. But instead, I chose to think little of what he said and to go my own way. I wish I could tell you that my earthly father was the only one I have ever done that to. But, it would not be true. I have done the same thing to my Heavenly Father. Here is the danger. If we despise the chastening of God long enough, God may eventually just stop trying to correct us and let us go our own way. The worst day you will ever have in your life will be the day God stops knocking on your door because you have despised and rejected His chastening.

Fainting at His Chastening

Then shall they call upon me, but I will not answer; they shall seek me early, but they shall not find me: For that they hated knowledge, and did not choose the fear of the Lord: They would none of my counsel: they despised all my reproof. Therefore shall they eat of the fruit of their own way, and be filled with their own devices. (Proverbs 1:28-31)

The second wrong response we can make is fainting because of His chastening. Fainting comes from a word that means "to fall apart." God does not want you to quit; that is not the purpose of chastening. It is the devil who wants you to quit. He wants you to think, "There's no hope for you. You've gone too far. Look at the consequences of what you're suffering. There is no way back." Can I tell you something vitally important? That is a lie of the devil himself. There is always hope. The fact that God had to chasten you is not reason to quit. It is a reason to rejoice! First, chastening proves that you are His child. Second, it proves that God loves you so much that He has not given up on you. So do not faint when you are chastened.

I told you earlier about Dan, my friend from high school. He had such great potential for the Lord. The chastening and the consequences he received were severe and embarrassing. He married his girlfriend after they found out she was pregnant. They came to church for a while, but then David and I started noticing he was not coming on Wednesday nights. Soon, he started skipping Sunday nights. Before long, they were not coming to church at all. Every time we tried to talk to him, he threw up a barrier and would not listen. The chastening Dan received discouraged him, and he fainted.

When I was in college, I had another friend who ended up in exactly the same situation. While he was home for Christmas break, his girlfriend got pregnant. He dropped out of school, and they got married. He suffered the same chastening and embarrassment Dan had. But, instead of fainting, he went back to his home church. He placed himself under the pastor's counsel, and accepted church discipline for what he had done wrong. He stayed involved in the church. Today, that young man is pastoring an independent, fundamental Baptist church. What is the difference? He did not faint. He allowed the chastening to have the result God intended in his life. Your response when God chastens you determines your future.

Receiving His Chastening

The wrong responses to chastening are despising it and fainting because of it. But, there is a right response. Verse six says God chastens "every son whom he receiveth." The key to making the right response is found in our position—our relationship with God. After the chastening is done, God opens His arms wide and welcomes us back. He receives us.

The word that is used here carries the idea of acknowledging someone as a son. When we draw near to God, He draws near to us. He never holds the past over our heads. He forgives and forgets and receives us.

When the Prodigal Son returned him, he found that his father had been watching and waiting for his return. Instead of berating the boy for everything he had done wrong, the father threw a party! He brought out a new robe, a ring, shoes, and celebrated the return of his son. But, the son had to heed the chastening he received in the pigpen and choose not to faint. He had to come to the point where he was ready to return to his father. God perfectly chastens His children. He never gives us more than we can handle. He uses as much pressure as is required to achieve the result (and it pays for us to listen to Him early!) of correction in our lives. The prophet Isaiah talked to the people of Israel using a farming illustration.

For the fitches are not threshed with a threshing instrument, neither is a cart wheel turned about upon the cummin; but the fitches are beaten out with a staff, and the cummin with a rod. Bread corn is bruised; because he will not ever be threshing it, nor break it with the wheel of his cart, nor bruise it with his horseman. (Isaiah 28:27-28)

Most of us do not grow our own grain to make bread anymore, so this concept is not one we are used to seeing. But, the point of the passage is that the tool used to thresh the different grain is determined by how hard the grain is. With a soft grain like cummin, a lighter rod was used. With a tougher grain like spelt (fitches) a heavier staff was used. Neither received the grinding of a cart wheel. That was saved for the toughest grains. The condition of your heart determines how harsh the chastening you receive has to be to get your attention. The sooner we respond to God's judgment, the sooner we can return to His arms and be received back into a close relationship with Him. Do not faint when you are rebuked of the Lord. Do not turn away; do not despise what He is doing in your life. Instead, turn to Him and be received. The sky is the limit to how useful you can be for His glory when you respond properly to His chastening.

11. Enduring Adversity

"If ye endure chastening, God dealeth with you as with sons; for what son is he whom the father chasteneth not? But if ye be without chastisement, whereof all are partakers, then are ye bastards, and not sons. Furthermore we have had fathers of our flesh which corrected us, and we gave them reverence: shall we not much rather be in subjection unto the Father of spirits, and live? For they verily for a few days chastened us after their own pleasure; but he for our profit, that we might be partakers of his holiness. Now no chastening for the present seemeth to be joyous, but grievous: nevertheless afterward it yieldeth the peaceable fruit of righteousness unto them which are exercised thereby."
—Hebrews 12:7-11

Majoring in Faith in Adversity University

We have been talking about the chastening that God designs for our lives as part of the education process at the University of Adversity. Remember that you enrolled in that school the day you got saved, and you will be a student until you go to Heaven. Every student in this university majors in faith so that they can receive the good report described in Hebrews 11:39. I want to focus your attention now specifically on enduring adversity. It is not a guarantee. Some people do not. Notice the phrase in verse seven, "if ye endure." While some people fail the test, others succeed. Let us look at what happens in the lives of those who endure adversity.

A Heavy Load

First, if you endure, **you have remained under the load** that God has placed upon you in spite of its weight. The word *"endure"* means *"to remain under or to persevere."* We see this in the life of Joseph. He suffered horrible adversity from his own family, from Potiphar's wife, and even from those he helped while in prison. He was sold into slavery. He was falsely accused and thrown in jail. Yet, every where Joseph went, he obeyed God and the authorities he found himself serving. If Joseph had not remained under the weight, God would not have exalted him to the position in second of command in all of the land of Egypt. God richly blesses those who stay faithful while they attend the University of Adversity; those who do not cut classes and do not quit. Remain faithful under the load that God has placed upon you.

Second, if you endure, **you have not despised the chastening of the Lord.**

There may have been moments when you did not listen, but by and large, you have heeded when He has tried to get your attention. Mother knew when I was little, that going out to play rendered me temporarily deaf to her voice. I somehow did not ever seem to be able to hear her when she called me to come inside. So, she got a big bell to ring when she wanted me to come home. If I did not listen to the bell, Dad would come find me. If that happened, he stopped by the willow tree in the neighbor's yard. Curses on every willow tree! If nothing else would work, those willow switches improved my hearing dramatically.

As we have seen before, God progressively disciplines us—the more we resist, the harder He chastises us. How much better it is to listen the first time He calls and not despise His chastening!

Third, if you endure, **you have not fainted when you were rebuked.** I remember my first year of Bible college. I wanted to quit. I was taking a freshman Greek class that met four days a week. I could barely speak English, let alone Greek! I remember having to call my parents and tell them I had failed the first nine week session. I figured I might as well give up, and that I was never going to make it. But, my mother had already turned my bedroom into a sewing room, and she did not want to give it up! They rebuked me. They encouraged me. I did not quit. In fact, I ended up making straight A's in Greek. I could have fainted; but instead, I endured.

No Dropping out of Classes

Adversity makes you want to quit. You have adversity in your life because that is the way God designed it. Solomon said, *"If thou faint in the day of adversity, thy strength is small."* (Proverbs 24:10) Many times, I have quoted that verse to myself and said, "God give me greater strength. I don't want to quit. I want to finish the course, keep the faith, and follow Your will for my life, so that I can receive a good report. Most of all, I want You to be pleased with my faith." I had this idea when I was younger that problems would peak, and then I would reach the point where my problems and pressures and hurts would decrease. It has not happened yet! And I have reached the point at 55 that I do not think it is ever going to happen because God wants to stretch me. Do you want to run the distance? Then, you must not faint in the adversity. You have to stay at it.

Fourth, if you endure, **God is dealing with you**. When verse seven says God *"dealeth with you,"* it is talking about "leaning in for a closer look." It is kind of like the teacher coming to your desk in school and leaning over and giving you personal help. God deals with you on a personal basis. We have talked before about Joseph, but let's look at his brothers for a moment. They hated Joseph, cast him into a pit, ignored his cries for help, sold him into slavery, and lied to Jacob to make him think Joseph was dead. It took more than twenty years of God dealing with them to get them to the point of reconciliation. When they went to Egypt to buy grain during the famine, Joseph had their money put back into their bags. When they opened their bags on the return trip, they knew they were in trouble. *"And they were afraid, saying one to another, What is this that God hath done unto us?"* (Genesis 42:28)

Notice that they did not say, "What an awful coincidence." There are no coincidences for a Christian. They recognized that God was working and active in their lives. But, it took years of enduring great affliction before they came to the position where they acknowledged that God was dealing with them. They eventually realized that their adversity was the result of what they had done against God and against Joseph. It is a wonderful thing when you reach the point where rather than griping and complaining or fainting in the day of adversity; instead you say, "God is dealing with me." When you are chastened, look to identify what area of your life God is trying to change—and make the change. Recognizing His purpose behind your adversity helps you endure.

Fifth, if you endure, **you are experiencing something every child needs**. The writer of Hebrews asks a rhetorical question here. *"What son is he whom the father chasteneth not?"* Parents who love their children chasten and correct them because every child needs correction. David said, *"The wicked are estranged from the womb: they go astray as soon as they be born, speaking lies."* (Psalm 58:3) If we, as parents, allow our children to do whatever they want, we are not going to lead to a life of success and contentment and joy. Instead, this life leads to rebellion and frustration and anger. It is the same for our Heavenly Father. He knows that we need to be corrected.

Purpose for Adversity University

So many times I have heard the question, "Preacher, why did this happen to me?" In fact, sometimes it is the preacher himself asking the question. June 3, 1988, will always be an important day in my own personal development in faith. That day, a very special daughter came into our lives; but initially, the circumstances seemed to be grossly unfair to me because of my misunderstanding of chastening. I had always considered chastening to be exclusively for the purpose of disciplining for disobedience.

Dianne, my dear wife who was pregnant and overdue, had been going in and out of labor for more than two weeks, and yet our sixth child was not cooperating though everything seemed normal. On a Friday afternoon, labor commenced once again; and with the aid of medicine, it was inevitable that the baby would be born soon. As the hospital's monitors registered my wife's vital signs as well as the heartbeat of our unborn infant, suddenly the beating of our baby's heart stopped! In a few moments, the hospital room was crowded with nurses; and I followed as a team of calm, but concerned, medical personnel took my wife down a hall and through the doors into a labor and delivery room. Here, a caesarean section was performed and a breathless, deep purple in color, and wrinkled-skinned daughter was delivered. Initial efforts to clear the little one's airways were unsuccessful, and we watched helplessly as she was whisked away for lifesaving treatment.

"Your child is alive," the doctor reported to us after a few minutes that seemed like a lifetime, "but she was without oxygen for several minutes, and is in very critical condition." I am embarrassed to say that, as I leaned against the labor and delivery wall, aware that my wife and I were entering into an adversity that would prove to be extremely painful, I angrily asked God what I had done to deserve this punishment. I did not see the wonderful purposes for adversity that our heavenly Father had in mind for us. Blessings were wrapped up in a little bundle of handicapped humanity, and I did not realize it!

In fact, when the nurse came to inquire the name we had selected for our daughter, my wife, then in recovery with me at her side, told the woman that her name would be called Janelle. "She will not be called Janelle", I said. "Janelle means 'gift from God,' and this is no gift from God." That morning, Dianne and I had read Proverbs 3 together, and there in that hospital ward she reproved my bad spirit by asking me to quote verses five and six together with her. Perhaps, our sixth child was, and is to this day, very appropriately called Janelle as she is truly a gift from God.

Adversity always has positive purposes but we must look for them by faith and seek to take advantage of the gift of adverse circumstances presented to us by our perfect University President Whose name is God. We may not know all of the reasons for difficult courses in our schooling in AU, but the Bible tells us two things that we can count on in considering God's purposes for adversity. Romans 8:28, a verse we know well, tells us that all things work together for good. Good for what? The answer is in verse 29. First, so that we would become like Jesus Christ--"conformed to the image of his Son." God wants us to be like His Son. Second, so that people will be saved—"the firstborn among many brethren." God wants us to draw others to Him. It is good that all things are working together to accomplish His will in our lives.

Every child of God receives His chastening because God is committed to His purpose that we be conformed to be like His Son, and that we be a witness of Christ to the world in which we live.

By the way, twenty years have passed since that monumental initiation into raising a legally blind and mentally handicapped child, and I am not sure that I can accurately assess whether or not I am more like Christ today than at that time, but I would like to believe that the Lord has used this child, Janelle, to move me forward in my walk with the Lord and into His likeness. As to the evangelistic issue, I can speak with wonderful accuracy of the many doctors, nurses, therapists, parents of children with cerebral palsy, and others who have come to Christ through the contacts we have made as a result of Janelle's presence in our lives.

Adversity Proves Relationship

Sixth, if we endure, **our relationship to God is proved**. So many people today have a false idea of their relationship with God. Many people think that because they go to church, or because they give, or because they live in America, or because they try hard to do good to others, that indicates they are a child of God. However, verse eight gives us a clear (if painful) test of whether we are truly Christians. "*But if ye be without chastisement, whereof all are partakers, then are ye bastards, and not sons.*" Chastening proves my relationship to God. I know I am saved. I have confidence in the Word and promises of God. But, I also know that I am saved because God chastens me.

People who are unsaved do experience adversity in life, but it is never from the switch of God. He does not chasten those who are not His own. Remember that willow tree I told you about? My dad never did take a willow switch after Danny or Mike or any of my other friends.

Their conduct and behavior and maturity were not his responsibility. He and Mom had plenty of exercise spanking Barbara, Marsha, Richard, and me. We were their children, and we never doubted that relationship. Let me ask you a vital question: Does God chasten you? There is nothing more important than knowing that you know that you belong to Christ—that you are saved. No adversity that you experience in this life will compare to the pain and suffering of an eternity separated from God in Hell. If you are not certain you are saved, trust Christ as your Savior today and get that matter settled forever.

12. REACHING YOUR POTENTIAL

"And ye have forgotten the exhortation which speaketh unto you as unto children,

My son, despise not thou the chastening of the Lord, nor faint when thou art

rebuked of him: For whom the Lord loveth he chasteneth, and scourgeth every

son whom he receiveth. If ye endure chastening, God dealeth with you as with

sons; for what son is he whom the father chasteneth not? But if ye be without

chastisement, whereof all are partakers, then are ye bastards, and not sons.

Furthermore we have had fathers of our flesh which corrected us, and we gave

them reverence: shall we not much rather be in subjection unto the Father of

spirits, and live? For they verily for a few days chastened us after their own

pleasure; but he for our profit, that we might be partakers of his holiness. Now

no chastening for the present seemeth to be joyous, but grievous: nevertheless

afterward it yieldeth the peaceable fruit of righteousness unto them which are

exercised thereby." —Hebrews 12:5-11

Know Pain; Know Gain

What do Colorado Springs, Colorado; Lake Placid, New York; and Chula Vista, California have in common? Each of these cities is home to a United States Olympic training center. Our athletes train there in preparation for the Olympic Games. In 2008, the 29th modern Olympics saw more than 10,000 athletes from around the world compete in more than 300 events in Beijing, China. We see the performance and the medals. What we do not see, but what lies behind every performance are the unseen, unnoticed, unknown trainers and training, countless hours, and rigorous discipline. All of that effort is designed to the athlete to be the very best he or she can be in representing our country.

Even though I am never going to be in the Olympics, and I do not live in Colorado Springs, Lake Placid, or Chula Vista, I am in training. God is the ultimate trainer for every believer. Just as it is in the Olympics, our performance in the Christian life is directly connected to the training we have endured. If we will endure the chastening, the correcting, and the training that God has for us and respond to it properly, we then can reach our potential for God. Without that training, we will be limited in our accomplishments for Him.

In Bible times, it was common for fathers to train their sons to take over their business. It was a generational norm in that society. So, the author of Hebrews uses that practice as the illustration of how God teaches and trains His children. He brings people, problems, pressures, and pain into our lives so that we can achieve our potential. In the athletic world, they say, "No pain; no gain." There is no progress without adversity. God says, "Know pain; know gain." He brings chastening into our lives to teach and train us. It is designed for the specific purpose of helping us reach His goal for us. Reaching your full potential for God requires that you understand the principles behind His training program.

"More" is Needed

At the beginning of verse nine, we see the word "furthermore." **In order to increase and go further, you must have more**. Your potential can only be reached if you are willing to go further and endure more.

If you endure more affliction, then you will go further. If you are only willing to endure less affliction, you cannot go as far. As God looks at your potential and mine, He brings circumstances and specific situations into our lives that are designed to help us reach His goal for us. Not every athlete has the same training program. They perform exercises that are tailored to the strengths they need to succeed in their individual sports. If we remain faithful under those adversities and submit to God in them, He will take us further in our lives. The moment that we cease to allow God to chasten us—when we quit, give up, or take it casually, we are limiting our ultimate potential for God. We must have more chastening—more training—to go further and reach our potential.

Past, Present, Future Training

We also see in this passage the perspective on our training program. God's training began in the past (*we have had fathers*), continues now (*chastening for the present*), and will produce results in the future (*afterward*). We must learn to step back and to take the broader view of what is happening in life. If you judge your life solely based on what is happening at this moment, or what happened in the past, then you are failing to see the perspective God wants you to see. He wants us to understand to the purpose behind the pressure. The "peaceable fruit of righteousness" only comes as the end result of the training process.

I have been working on getting in better shape. I received a treadmill as a gift and put it in the basement. It has about ten different settings. I can do different speeds or incline the track to increase the difficulty. If I set it on the lowest level and only use that, I get a little benefit, but I am missing out on a lot. If I take on the next setting—a little more incline, a little faster pace, a little longer session—my benefit increases. That only happens if I endure the pain. The path of least resistance never leads to great success in life. In his poem "The Ladder of Saint Augustine," Henry Wadsworth Longfellow wrote:

> *The heights by great men reached and kept*
> Were not attained through sudden flight,
> *But they while their companions slept*
> *Were toiling upward through the night.*

Early Development

The second principle that we see here is that **the sooner we begin, the greater our accomplishment will be.** There is a reason for the focus here on fathers and childhood. Setting the course early in life allows us much more time to grow and learn and serve God. Evangelist D. L. Moody once told a pastor that he had seen two and a half people saved in the last service. The pastor asked, "Two adults and one child?" Moody replied, "No. Two children and one adult. The adult only has half a life left to give to God." Good habits developed in youth lead to greater potential in our adult years.

The devil knows this, so he tries to get us to believe a lie. "You're young. Don't worry about those spiritual things right now. Now is the time to go ahead and have your fun. Don't take things too seriously. After all, when you're older you will have plenty of time to get right with God, and then you can serve Him." There is a price to pay for wasted years, and that price is wasted potential. You say, "But I can't go back to the past." You're absolutely right. So, rather than be depressed over lost opportunities, the best thing you can do is start in the present right where you are today. Someone once said, "A wasted life is nothing but a collection of wasted days." There will never be a better time to enter training, than right now.

Multiple Trainers

Next, notice the comparison that is drawn between our earthly fathers and our Heavenly Father. **There are many trainers, but only one Master.** Often, we do not appreciate the people who correct us, especially in our youth and immaturity. But, we need to be grateful for every individual that God has placed into our lives in a place of leadership. He has ordained them to inspire and challenge and coerce and compel and press us to become all that we can be for God. They are working for our benefit to help us reach our potential. They are trainers working under the Master Trainer toward the same goal and purpose. The circumstances and people God brings into our lives are intended to train us.

There are three unmistakable evidences that we have the right attitude toward our trainers. The first is **_being correctable_**. If our first response is "Who do they think they are to tell me that?" Then, you have not got the concept. That is evidence of rebellion against God. It shows that you have not made the connection between the people in your life, in leadership, in authority and God, the Father in Heaven. The second is **_showing respect_**. Verse nine says we are to give our fathers "*reverence*," or respect. If your attitude is one of resentment rather than respect, then you are in danger of derailing your training.

You are not likely to listen to a coach you do not respect. Finally, we see the evidence of **_subjection._** Your willingness to submit to authority is a statement that you understand this principle. Your parents, employer, teachers, and pastors are resources—provided that you submit yourself to their authority and allow them to give you the guidance that you need.

An Important Expulsion

While a student in a Christian university, one of our sons was expelled for what some would consider a minor infraction of the rules. His call to inform his mother and me of the situation was difficult; however, as his parents, we saw an opportunity for our child to cease from pursuing a relationship with a female classmate that we knew was not God's choice for his life partner. His response to the "trainers" at school and at home would be critical to his future development in faith.

Although he had a car at school and could have driven home alone, our nineteen-year-old teen, embarrassed and discouraged, asked if I could come there and accompany him—a request which would mean missing a Sunday in my pulpit. My answer of "yes" to his request was received with surprise and gladness as he knew the importance of church ministry to his pastor and father. I explained to him that my family is also my ministry and his needs were of greater priority to me than any public responsibility. Unwittingly, placing my parental duty above my pastoral responsibility became a key factor in our child accepting the adversity of being expelled from college and submitting to his parent's wishes. Our three-day trip together was mightily used of God to grow and mature our offspring in helping him to pass this course in Adversity University.

When his girlfriend and her parents called several days later and asked our son to consider a move to their community for the purpose of advancing the courtship of their daughter and our son, he refused. "I am not going to disobey my parents whom God has set over me for my protection," he told them. His attitude of being correctable, respectful, and submissive through this adversity eventually led to meeting, dating, and marrying an incredible Christian lady and to a career and ministry that is being greatly blessed of the Lord.

The fourth principle is **the priority of the spiritual over the**

physical. The contrast is drawn between the "fathers of our flesh" and "the Father of spirits." There are many people who give of their time and energy sacrificially to become better physically, emotionally, or mentally. Those are all good things, but if we neglect the spiritual part of our lives, then we stunt our potential growth for God. Paul told Timothy, *"For bodily exercise profiteth little: but godliness is profitable unto all things, having promise of the life that now is, and of that which is to come."* (I Timothy 4:8) He did not say the physical had no value; just that its value was temporal and less important than a focus on godliness. The spiritual dimension of life is of far greater importance than any other aspect.

We demonstrate our understanding of this concept by how we order our priorities. Is there time for church? Do you daily read the Bible, making it your own personal book to study, meditate on, memorize, learn, and implement in your life? Do you seek to do God's will? When we understand the importance of the spiritual dimension of our lives, it increases the potential of our lives. The spiritual aspect gives us the ability to continue to grow and develop. Even in our older years, when our physical abilities inevitably decline, we can continue to grow spiritually.

Attitude Determines Altitude

I am sure you have seen two teams competing against each other that had similar talent, similar ability, similar training, yet one excels over the other. The difference is usually found in the team's spirit—their belief and confidence in their coaches and their training. Attitude is a great determining factor in altitude. The famous college football coach Bear Bryant said, "If you believe in yourself and have dedication and pride—and never quit—you'll be a winner. The price of victory is high, but so are the rewards." You and I may have great talent, and we may have great ability; but if our attitude stinks, then our potential is going to be diminished greatly.

Fifth, we need to remind ourselves that **our perspective will improve as we look back from the future**. Verse ten says our earthly fathers chasten us *"for a few days."* It sure does not seem like a few days when you are young. I can remember waiting for Christmas when I was little. On December 1, when Christmas was 24 days away, those 24 days seemed like a lifetime. Now, 24 days seems like the steam coming off of a cup of coffee. Your perspective improves as the present becomes the past. Do not quit because your circumstances are challenging right now. As you grow and mature, the problems that you are facing now are going to seem much smaller than they do today.

Remember the story of David and Goliath? When King Saul asked David how he could face a giant trained in the arts of war, David told him about the lion and the bear that God had helped him kill while he was tending sheep. When we look back at all the victories He has helped us win, our perspective on adversity changes. Somebody mentioned a problem to me and asked, "Are you worried about that?" I said, "There was a day when I would have worried, but I have got bigger fish to fry than that now." I look back now on situations in my youth that seemed overwhelming to me, and see that they were not really as bad as I thought they were at the time. I think of the pressures and problems I had as a young husband, then as a dad, and a new pastor, and I look at how much they made me grow.

If you do not grow and develop, if you do not understand and mature, so that your view on the past and your perspective on it changes, then you will spend your life in discouragement. Every person who has come into my life and everything that has ever happened to me was designed by God to develop me so that I could reach my potential. I look back, and I can say, "You know what? Thank God for those circumstances. Thank God for those people." I was not always happy about it at the time, but I can see the purpose and plan behind it all now.

Chastening Profits our Potential

Next, we see that **the pain of chastening is for our profit**. Often, it is hard to see the reason while we are suffering the adversity. Joseph endured decades before he was able to look back and see God's design in everything that had happened to him. He told his brothers, *"But as for you, ye thought evil against me; but God meant it unto good, to bring to pass, as it is this day, to save much people alive."* (Genesis 50:20)

Dianne and I have been married thirty-four years. We have had a part in the lives of twelve children. Was it easy? Absolutely not. Was it a lot of work? Absolutely. Was there a lot of sacrifice to have Dianne stay at home to be there with the kids? Sure. But, was it worth it? Absolutely. There is a profit that only comes from enduring the pain. I am enjoying now in my mid-50's, the profit of enduring my 30's and 40's, and I do not want to forfeit that. Are there still challenges? Absolutely. God has more lessons He wants me to learn. But I am enjoying today the blessings of enduring the past. Stay with it; endure God's chastening. Eventually, you will see the profit that you received from enduring the pain.

Ultimate Potential

Finally, we see that our ultimate potential is realized in *who we become,* rather than *in what we accomplish.* Verse ten tells us God's supreme goal and purpose behind every adversity He brings into our lives—*"that we might be partakers of his holiness."* It is all designed to help us become like Jesus Christ. Ultimately, God's goals for our lives are not about what we can do for Him, but what He can do in us. You will not reach all of your goals. That's a good thing. The poet Robert Browning wrote, "A man's reach should exceed his grasp, or what's a heaven for?" But, as you grow and mature in the Lord, you will have a growing contentment with what God is doing in your life that far exceeds any trophies that could ever be given to you.

What the training camp of life is really all about for the Christian is not to go to an Olympic event to win and get a gold or silver or bronze medal. The ultimate goal is what the training accomplishes in the life of the athlete. The training that God has prepared and brought into your life and mine is designed to change you and me to become more and more like Jesus Christ. If I do not achieve any other grand goal that I might have, but that goal is realized, then I have reached my potential. That is God's purpose for my life...and yours. He planned it and predestined it before we were ever born.

And we know that all things work together for good to them that love God, to them who are the called according to his purpose. For whom he did foreknow, he also did predestinate to be conformed to the image of his Son, that he might be the firstborn among many brethren. (Romans 8:28-29)

13. THE KEY TO SURVIVAL

"Furthermore we have had fathers of our flesh which corrected us, and we gave them reverence: shall we not much rather be in subjection unto the Father of spirits, and live?" —Hebrews 12:9

A Matter of Life and Death

There is a serious question and a stern warning for us in this verse. This is not simply a metaphor; it is not an allegory; it is real. If we are not in subjection to the Father, then we cannot expect to live. Many Christians fail to properly recognize God's chastening; others recognize that God is chastening, but they respond with rebellion instead of responding biblically. Either way, the results are the same. If we are not in subjection to the Father of spirits, we cannot live. Our culture, our churches, and most Christians have lost the concept of the fear of the Lord.

"For if we sin willfully after that we have received the knowledge of the truth, there remaineth no more sacrifice for sins, But a certain fearful looking for of judgment and fiery indignation, which shall devour the adversaries. He that despised Moses' law died without mercy under two or three witnesses: Of how much sorer punishment, suppose ye, shall he be thought worth, who hath trodden under foot the Son of God, and hath counted the blood of the covenant, wherewith he was sanctified, an unholy thing, and hath done despite unto the Spirit of grace? For we know him that hath said, Vengeance belongeth unto me, I will recompense, saith the Lord. And again, The Lord shall judge his people. It is a fearful thing to fall into the hands of the living God." (Hebrews 10:26-31)

This warning is not given for the unsaved. It is true that God will judge the lost. However, the author of Hebrews says *"the Lord shall judge his people."* It is a warning to those of us who are children of God that we take God's chastening seriously in our lives. That requires first that we recognize God's chastening. Not everything that goes wrong is God's judgment, because we live in a fallen world filled with sin. But, we should always be diligent to examine ourselves and see if we are being chastened. Then, we must properly respond by repenting and forsaking the sin for which we are being chastened. This is literally a matter of life and death. In 1 Corinthians 11:30, Paul wrote, *"For this cause* [speaking of people eating the Lord's Supper unworthily] *many are weak and sickly among you, and many sleep."*

According to Hebrews 12:9, the key to responding properly to God's chastening is found in submitting ourselves to the Heavenly Father. What does it mean to be in subjection to Him? The Greek word translated "subjection" is *hupotasso* which was a military term, meaning to arrange in order under the command of the leader. Subjection to God means placing ourselves under His authority. It means that we take care of the problem His chastening is bringing to our attention instead of being bitter and refusing to listen. So, the first thing we see in this verse is the relationship between chastening and submission, and this principle applies on many different levels.

Personal Judgment

First, **this principle is applicable personally**. All of us need God's chastening because all of us struggle with right thinking and with right actions. As a result, our God who knows us personally, intimately and is observing every step of our lives and every thought of our minds, chastens us. He does not chasten us because He is an ogre who is out to destroy us. He chastens us because He loves us too much to allow sin to remain in our lives. He knows us perfectly; and based on His knowledge, everyone and everything He brings into our lives is designed by Him for our good. When we respond to Him properly, we experience life as it was meant to be lived.

When was the last time you recognized that God was chastening you? When I got a spanking from my dad, I never had to wonder, "Did anything happen here?" No, I knew exactly what happened. I knew who gave me the spanking, and I knew why he gave it to me. Do you think our perfect Heavenly Father would not make provision for us to recognize when He is chastening us? The problem is not that He is not communicating it; the problem is that we are not listening. Things happen to us, and we respond just like the world. We chalk it up to Murphy's Law, or we say, "Well, that's just the way things happen." Again, not everything that goes wrong is chastening, but God does chasten every one of His children. Knowing that truth, when we experience trouble, we need to examine our lives to see if there is anything that needs to change. The problem many people have is that they do not want to change, so they try to ignore the chastening hand of God to avoid repenting of their sin. They do not want to acknowledge what is happening as chastening because that would force them to deal with the sin.

Effects on the Family

Second, **this principle is applicable to the family**. God designed the family unit from the beginning. The family relationship is the foundation of society. God works with families as well as individuals. What I think and do as a father in responding to chastening has implications for my wife and children. In the military, they talk about something called collateral damage—when something or somebody that was not the target gets hit. Parents and children alike can cause a lot of grief, sorrow, heartache, and hurt to the family when they do not recognize and respond to God's chastening properly. That brings down God's judgment.

One of the greatest missionary heroes in history was Jonathan Goforth. He and his wife, Rosalind, were pioneer missionaries to China in the 1800's. The hardships of the mission field were great; and after years of struggle, Rosalind asked her husband to build her a home like the one they had left behind in Canada in the city so that she could remain there while he traveled and preached. She was tired of the suffering. In her wonderful book *How I Know God Answers Prayer*, she told how her husband, with grave misgivings agreed to do what she asked. "Dearest, I fear what God is going to do," he said. They finished the house and he returned to the mission work. Just a few days later, their youngest child got sick and died. She wrote, "God was chastening me. I repented of my sin. I re-surrendered my life to God. We sold the house with the picket fence, and I went back to field with my husband, serving the Lord." God applies His chastening to families.

Effects on the Church

Third, **this principle is applicable to churches**. The church is the body of Christ. If one member allows sin in his life, it does not just impact and influence that individual, it affects the entire church. The story of Achan is a vivid reminder of this truth. Joshua told the people they were not allowed to take any spoils from the capture of Jericho; everything in the city belonged to God. But Achan took gold, silver, and clothing and hid it in his tent. As a result, Israel lost the battle of Ai, and thirty-six soldiers were killed. Sin does not stay contained; what you allow in your life will have a dramatic effect on the body of

Christ—the local church of which you are a part.

As I have traveled and preached and tried to help other ministries, I have seen that not every fundamental, Bible-believing church is doing well. Some of them are struggling. Just believing the right things is not enough; we also have to do the right things. There are churches today that are experiencing divine chastening. When churches refuse to properly respond to God's chastening, the same thing happens that happens to individuals—they stop living. John wrote, *"And unto the angel of the church in Sardis write; These things sayeth he that hath the seven Spirits of God, and the seven stars; I know thy works, that thou hast a name that thou livest, and art dead."* (Revelation 3:1) What is the church? It is not a building; it is us! When we live cavalierly, not caring about what God is trying to tell us, it brings judgment on the church.

Effects on our City

Fourth, **this principle is applicable to cities.** When we think of cities and sin, most of us immediately think of Sodom and Gomorrah. Did God chasten those cities? Yes. Before they were destroyed, He allowed enemies to conquer them. Abraham had to take his army of servants to rescue Lot and the other inhabitants of Sodom and Gomorrah and return their possessions. That was God's chastening; but because they did not heed it, eventually, they lost their lives. Do you think God has changed His attitude toward sin? He still hates pride, gluttony, laziness, cold-heartedness and sodomy (Ezekiel 16:49-50) just as much now as He did then.

Do you think that the same God who judged Sodom will judge sin today? Where do we find the highest crime rates in America? Is it in the places where God is ignored the most, or in the places where He is listened to the most? If we do not heed His chastening in our cities, we can expect destruction. What part of America has suffered the most in recent years? The terrorists killed thousands in New York City on 9/11. Hurricane Katrina devastated New Orleans in 2005. The city that has been hit the hardest economically by the housing crisis is Las Vegas. Those are some of the most wicked parts of our nation—cities in which a vast majority of people do not live according to the laws of God. I am not saying that bad things do not happen in other places, or that all of the people who suffered from those tragic events were wicked. What I am saying is that God chastens cities, and we need to listen when He calls us to repentance.

Affects on our Country

Finally, **this principle is applicable to our country**. Recently, I read Joel Rosenberg's book *Epicenter: Why the Current Rumblings in the Middle East Will Change your Future*. It was an eye-opening reminder to me that God does indeed judge and chasten nations. He traces the work of terrorists and governments of countries like Iran that hate America, and predicts that we are going to see further attacks right here in the United States. Rosenberg, who was raised as an Orthodox Jew before becoming a Christian, first became famous because nine months before 9/11, he wrote a novel that began with Muslim terrorists hijacking airplanes to attack America's cities. He clearly sees God at work in chastening our nation, and believes the Bible.

I do not know what is going to happen. But, I know that *"whom the Lord loveth he chasteneth, and scourgeth every son whom he receiveth."* Why should God not bring judgment on our land? Did we heed the chastening of 9/11? Did we turn from our wicked ways and seek His face? No. We were shocked by the terrorists' attacks, but not shocked enough to recognize God's chastening and respond properly and begin submission to His Word. The devil wants to keep us out of the Bible. He does not want us to recognize God's divine training, or His chastening in our lives. He does not want us to respond to God by repentance and submitting unto Him.

Spiritual Warfare

The second thing we see in this verse is the importance of understanding spiritual warfare. God is referred to as *"the Father of spirits."* This is the only time in Scripture that we see God described this way. In order to properly respond to His chastening, we have to understand His relationship to the spirit world. The "spirits" talked about here are the angels—both those loyal to God and those loyal to Satan. There is an unseen spiritual warfare going on all around us. The devil wants us to think that every thing that is going on in our lives is just about us. He wants us to ignore the spiritual warfare aspect of our lives.

Throughout His ministry here on earth, Christ was constantly facing opposition from demons. The Bible teaches us that there are different levels of authority in the spiritual world. Paul wrote, *"Put on the whole armour of God, that ye may be able to stand against the wiles of the devil. For we wrestle not against flesh and blood, but against principalities, against powers, against the rulers of the darkness of this world, against spiritual wickedness in high places."* (Ephesians 6:11-12) We have a mayor in Rockford. The state of Illinois has a governor. And the United States has a president. Just as there are different levels of authority in the physical world, there are levels of authority in the devil's realm.

Understand that though they are powerful and very active in our world, they are not in control. Because God is the Father of spirits, He determines what they are able to do; and God does sometimes use demonic powers to chasten His children. Now, there are some people who look for demons under every rock. We can over-focus on this truth of spiritual warfare. But just as Jesus had to deal with these powers in His day, we have to expect them to still be working in our day. Satan wants you to think, "I'm jealous because of what she did." But the Bible says there is a spirit—a demonic power—of jealousy. If we yield to it, it will make us jealous. I am not talking about being possessed, because that is impossible for a believer. But, we can allow ourselves to be influenced by these forces of evil. That is what happened to King Saul. First Samuel 16 tells us that because He refused to heed God's chastening, *"an evil spirit from the Lord troubled him."* (I Samuel 16:14) God allowed a demonic spirit to trouble Saul. That spirit made him angry and jealous. Because Saul was not yielding to God's desire for his life, God chastened him through the unseen spirit world. If you study what the Bible says about evil spirits, there are a number of them. We can be attacked by a spirit of slumber (Romans 11:28) that can place us in a state of spiritual sleep. Isaiah 61:3 talks about a spirit of heaviness. This is the word for what we call depression. If you are depressed because you are disobedient to God, and a spirit of depression has been allowed to make you depressed, then all of the pills and psychoanalysis in the world is not going to help. Repenting of your sin and getting right with God is the only course you can take.

I am not saying that every problem is caused by demonic spirits. But, we need to be alert to the potential impact of spiritual warfare. Over the years, we have worked with people who were gripped by immorality. The Bible says there is a spirit of whoredoms. (Hosea 4:12) Some people (certainly not everyone) are sick because of a spirit of infirmity. (Luke 13:11) There are spirits of bondage and fear—the list goes on and on. We need to be alert and aware to the spiritual warfare going on in our lives. If we are struggling, we need to see if evil spirits are out to destroy, to wreck, to ruin, our personal faith, our personal lives, our families, our churches, our communities, and our nation. If we do not consider this reality, we may tragically miss out on recognizing and responding to God's chastening.

14. THREE REASONS FOR PAINFUL CHASTENING

"And ye have forgotten the exhortation which speaketh unto you as unto children,

My son, despise not thou the chastening of the Lord, nor faint when thou art

rebuked of him: For whom the Lord loveth he chasteneth, and scourgeth every

son whom he receiveth. If ye endure chastening, God dealeth with you as with

sons; for what son is he whom the father chasteneth not? But if ye be without

chastisement, whereof all are partakers, then are ye bastards, and not sons.

Furthermore we have had fathers of our flesh which corrected us, and we gave

them reverence: shall we not much rather be in subjection unto the Father of

spirits, and live? For they verily for a few days chastened us after their own

pleasure; but he for our profit, that we might be partakers of his holiness.

—Hebrews 12:5-10

Life is Difficult

No matter who you are, whether you are saved or unsaved, life is difficult. If you are unsaved, your life is difficult because you do not have the Lord Jesus Christ in your life. If you are saved, your life is difficult because you do have the Lord Jesus Christ in your life. If you got saved thinking your life would not be difficult any more, you were wrong. Whether you are saved or unsaved, life is difficult and full of trouble. Now, for the unsaved, there is no hope. At the end of the road is Hell—a lake of fire forever and ever. For the saved, we can look forward to a better land. But, throughout life, we are going to be dealing with pain and struggle and difficulty; and for those of us who are saved, the chastening hand of God. In Hebrews 12:10, we see three purposes that lie behind the chastening we receive.

Reason of Pleasure

First, **chastening is for pleasure**. *"For they verily for a few days chastened us after their own pleasure."* Now at first glance, this seems to be rather strange. In fact, chastening someone for pleasure sounds sadistic and sick. But, God is not evil and sadistic. He does not take pleasure in the fact that we are being chastened; the pleasure is because He knows that chastening has divine blessing and benefit as its end result. If we are going to become what our Father intends for us to be, then He must allow us to experience pain. He takes pleasure, not in our the pain, but in what it will produce.

To help you understand this, let's look at the times God the Father said He was pleased with His Son Jesus. The first was when Jesus was baptized. After John baptized Jesus, a voice from Heaven said, *"This is my beloved Son, in whom I am well pleased."* (Matthew 3:17) What was it about Christ's baptism that pleased the Father? Baptism is a picture of the death, burial, and resurrection of Christ. The Father was looking ahead to the suffering of His Son. The second time was on the Mount of Transfiguration. Jesus was talking to Moses and Elijah about His soon coming death. Peter, James, and John heard a voice from Heaven that said, *"This is my beloved Son, in whom I am well pleased."* (Matthew 17:5)

Was the Father pleased when Jesus worked miracles and preached the gospel? Yes, He was. In John 8:29 Jesus said, *"I do always those things that please him."* The expression of God's pleasure focused on Jesus' obedient suffering. God was not pleased in seeing His Son hurt, but He was pleased in seeing His Son's obedience and His willingness to suffer unselfishly for the sake of others.

There are some lessons that we are not likely to learn in sermons; we learn them through suffering. We are born naturally selfish. If you have children, you know that our nature is "Me first." Kids do not have to go to school and take Selfishness 101—it comes naturally. The only way to overcome that trait is to be broken through God's divine chastening. Selfish people make poor husbands, poor wives, poor workers, and poor Christians. Chastening helps us to learn to please others rather than focusing on what pleases us.

A few years ago, my family and I had the privilege of seeing Rachel Barton, the world-renowned violinist from Chicago at a concert. When she came on to the stage, it was obvious that she walked with a severe limp. With great difficulty, she made her way to her seat and began to play. I have never heard anyone else play with such emotion, beauty, and grace. We sat spellbound as we listened to her. Later, I found out her story. When she was in her early twenties, Rachel was getting off a train to teach violin lessons carrying her 400 year old Amati violin worth more than half a million dollars. The door of the train closed on her shoulder and caught the violin case. She was dragged more than 350 feet by the train. One leg was severed, and the other was badly injured. Rachel Barton could have given up. Instead, she continues to practice and play through the pain for the pleasure of others. Every pain that God brings or allows into our lives has a purpose. If we respond to it properly, that purpose will be accomplished. When we enduring chastening for the pleasure of others, it pleases God.

Reason of Profit

Second, **chastening is for profit**. *"But he for our profit."* Personal profit or benefit is only realized following pain. Now, I know we are living in a world that does not want to believe that. People want a pill they can take to eat all they want and still lose weight. We want great relationships without having to make any investments in them. There is no free lunch. As athletes say, "No pain, no gain." There is no way to get paid in advance in the spiritual realm. You cannot get the profit unless you endure the pain. God says if we endure chastening, then we will be rewarded. God will not do for us what we must do for ourselves.

Hebrews 11:6 says *"he that cometh to God."* God wants us to come to Him. Jesus said, *"Come unto me, all yet that labour and are heavy leaden, and I will give you rest."* (Matthew 11:28) Some people do not benefit from the Lord because they are not willing to come to Him. They are what I call "couch potato Christians." They just sit around, wanting everything to come to them. That is not the way God designed for us to work. In the Sermon on the Mount, Jesus said when people persecute and falsely attack, "Rejoice, and be exceeding glad." Now, most of us do not respond that way when we are having troubles. We do not jump up and down and click our heels and celebrate. But Jesus said that is how excited we should be. Why? Because we have a great reward in Heaven waiting for us! There is profit in chastening. If we endure the pain now, we get the profit later.

God brings pain and suffering into our lives because He loves us too much to let us sit back and expect people to take care of us. There is a mindset common in our country that says, "People owe me something. I'm just here to get what I can get. I deserve all I want." The only thing we deserve is to die and go to Hell. Anything else is only the result of God's grace and mercy. As a result of that spirit of entitlement, we have lost the work ethic that our parents and grandparents had; the idea that if you wanted to get ahead, you had to roll up your sleeves and get to work. The old farmers said, "The best place to pray for corn is at the end of a hoe handle."

You cross a boundary into a new level of maturity in your life when you can sincerely look to the Lord as He allows suffering and say, "Thank you, Father." If you are not being hypocritical about it, but mean it sincerely, then you have reached that level. The principle that we profit through pain is hard to learn in the classroom; instead God brings us into crisis. It is hard to gain this truth from academics; instead God brings us into adversity. And if we learn this truth, then we gain the reward that comes to those who endure chastening.

Reason of Partaking of God's Holiness

Third, **chastening is for partaking of God's holiness.** *"That we might be partakers of his holiness."* God saved the best reason for last. We see the word "partakers" twice in this passage; here in verse ten and also in verse eight. Though the same word is used in English, two different ideas are being expressed. In talking about the chastisement every Christian experiences, the word means "one's share as a participant." We are chastened because we have not yet attained perfection. We are going to be in Adversity University until we have breathed our last breath and God takes us home. The word "partakers" in verse ten is different; in fact, it is the same as in Acts 2:46 where it is translated "to eat."

Here is the distinction between the two words. Everyone who gets saved is invited into the training camp. They have a share of chastisement as a participant in the family of God. But only those who endure chastening get to sit down with the Lord and eat. Every believer is a partaking in His chastening; only those who endure are partakers of His holiness. When we are faced with adversity, we must run to God in faith. If we do not, we will quit. It is a tragedy to partake of the chastening without partaking of the holiness. That means we have suffered without gaining the purpose and benefit that was the intended purpose of our chastening.

An improper response to God's chastening will leave you thin and spiritually emaciated. When Karen Carpenter died in 1983, most of us had never heard of anorexia. It is a disorder that makes people quit eating. Refusing to endure chastening affects you the same way—you are giving up spiritual food. It will wreck and ruin your life. I have observed many Christians who lost their spiritual vitality during a time of adversity. They either ignored what God was doing, or they got angry at God and turned away from Him. Both are improper responses. They failed to see what God was trying to do in their lives. Ultimately, the best and greatest profit of chastening is that it allows us to be partakers of Christ's holiness. This means that we take on the very nature of Christ. When something is referred to as holy, it carries the idea of being perfectly cleansed.

Needed: Agitation

Think about the way a washing machine works. Open the lid while a load of clothes is being washed and look at it. There are clothes and water and soap in the machine, but they are not just sitting there. They do not get clean by simply being in the water. A washing machine has something that moves them around—an agitator. You will have to hold the little button down to watch it work with the lid open, but what you will see is the clothes are bouncing up and down, pulsating and spinning around. Do you have any agitations in your life? They are there to move things around so that you can be a partaker of His cleanness and holiness. God knows that without something to stir us up, we will not become more like His Son.

For the process to work though, you have to stay in the machine. The agitation may be painful, but it is necessary if you want to partake of Christ's holiness. If things are difficult and agitated in your marriage, stay in. If you are having a tough time at work, stay in. If there are troubles at your church, stay in. That agitation has been put in your life by God for a reason. If you get out, you will miss it. If we endure chastening, then one day we will be all cleaned up and presented to the Savior as a bride, spotless and white. Why? Because we made the decision, "I'm going to endure chastening. I'm going to stay in the washing machine and endure the agitation. I'm not going to quit. I'm not going to give up. I'm not going to stay out just because things are tough. I'm going to stay in." Enduring chastening is easier if we keep in mind the purposes God has for having us go through it.

15. Experiencing Joy While Enduring Chastening

"Now no chastening for the present seemeth to be joyous, but grievous: nevertheless afterward it yieldeth the peaceable fruit of righteousness unto them which are exercised thereby." —Hebrews 12:11

Jump for Joy!

In the last chapter, we talked about God's purposes for chastening us. In this chapter, we take the next step into something that seems impossible—not just enduring chastening, but learning to enjoy it. I mentioned the Sermon on the Mount, and Jesus' instruction to rejoice when we are persecuted. The word literally means to jump for joy! That is not an easy thing to do. It goes against every natural tendency that we have. It is God's will that we experience joy even while enduring pain. When Paul and Silas were beaten and thrown into jail in Philippi, they could have been discouraged and defeated. They could have griped and complained, and we would say they would have been justified. But, that is not what they did. *"And at midnight Paul and Silas prayed, and sang praises unto God: and the prisoners heard them."* (Acts 16:25)

We have an early service on Sunday mornings at North Love. I have a tough enough time singing praises unto God at that time, let alone at midnight. These men of God were unfairly, mercilessly, stripped stark naked in front of a mob of people whom they had been preaching to, beaten harshly, and thrown into the innermost part of the prison. And they started singing praises to God! It is possible to experience joy even while enduring chastening.

Notice what our verse says—*"no chastening...seemeth to be joyous."* The point is not that chastening can't be joyous, but that if we only look at what is right in front of us, we will miss the possibility for joy. Things are not always as they seem. In fact, I would venture to say things are not ever as they seem. What we can see is not all that is occurring. We have a very limited view in the flesh of what is taking place. That is why faith is so important. Faith lets us see that God is at work behind the scenes in every circumstance. *"By faith he [Moses] forsook Egypt, not fearing the wrath of the king: for he endured, as seeing him who is invisible."* (Hebrews 11:27) And faith not only lets us see that God is at work; faith makes it possible for us to endure. The only way to experience joy in the midst of the chastening is if we recognize that which cannot be seen with the naked eye. The problem identified in Hebrews 12:11 is that we insist on supposing that things are as they seem to be. Our logic tells us this is the way it is. Our eyesight tells us this is the way it is. The world in which we live tells us this is the way it is. And, if we listen to logic and sight and the world, we miss out on what God has for us.

Faith Makes It Possible

First, **we must see by faith.** It is impossible to experience the joy of the Lord during chastening unless we are relying on faith to see past our circumstances. Joy is being filled with cheer (not happiness) and experiencing calm delight in the soul. We will never know joy if our focus is on the physical world we can see. Some people say that it is impossible to change our focus, but God never gives us an expectation that He does not enable us to fulfill. He says in I Thessalonians 5:16, *"Rejoice evermore."* There is no way around that one! It does not mean rejoice when we are in Heaven someday, it means rejoice right now here on earth.

My best friend from childhood became my brother-in-law and companion in pastoral ministry. I observed his great faith when he endured his last course in Adversity University, custom-designed for him. Several years after we both entered ministry, David (my wife Dianne's older brother) was diagnosed with colon cancer and joyfully endured the unfortunate spread of the disease to other organs of his body. At forty-three years of age, he was nearing the end of his life on earth when doctors discovered that his dear wife, Mary, was suffering from a malignant brain tumor which would, and did, take her life two years later.

The two weeks between discovering Mary's cancer and David's death were difficult for their four children and for each of us who loved this marvelous husband and wife; however, David could see (by faith) that God was in control. He knew that God did not make mistakes, and this attitude was conveyed consistently to all who were around him. His faith made it possible for him to experience joy while enduring his own cancer as well as the sorrow of his wife's terminal illness.

The evening before his home-going, I had taken their children off to their midweek service while Dianne cared for both her brother and her sister-in-law in their home.

Remarkably, though David had not eaten for a time, he removed his oxygen mask and asked Dianne for ice cream. Soon, my wife returned with three bowls of the requested dessert. While consuming the ice cream, her brother asked the name of the flavor. Now, Dianne did not want to tell her dying sibling the specific name of the ice cream, and so she said that it was chocolate. But, for some reason, David was not satisfied with the generic answer. He insisted that she tell him specifically what kind of chocolate ice cream he was eating. Sheepishly, she told him that he was eating "Death by Chocolate," the name of the flavor of ice cream, to which he laughed and said, "I don't know how it's affecting you, but this ice cream's killing me!"

The children and I arrived home at that moment and could not comprehend how two people (who were so near death) and their care-giving relative could be laughing with such intensity that they were crying. Their "Death by Chocolate" experience became a historic landmark in the lives of their soon-to-be-orphaned children. Dave and Mary's offspring observed their parents experiencing joy while enduring adversity. I can tell you that this made a tremendous impact in the lives of these four children. Faith in God made it possible.

Endure Chastening to Progress for the Lord

The most miserable Christians I know are those who despise the chastening of the Lord. They allow the circumstances of their suffering to make them miserable because they make the mistake of thinking and believing that things are as they seem to be. Even when things are going wrong and we are suffering, God is not dead. He has not abandoned us. He is very active and involved in our lives. That is the only way we can rejoice in chastening. I can choose to see what my eyes cannot see as well as believe that things are not as they seem to be. If we insist on living by what we can see (which is logical and makes sense), we forfeit the potential of joy, and we guarantee the presence of grief in our lives—it seems grievous, which means to be filled with sorrow and sadness. You will be de-energized, diminished, de-motivated, and depressed.

Notice the word "nevertheless" in verse eleven. What does 'nevertheless' mean? It means "always the more." How does that fit in with the context here? This passage is teaching us that it is only through enduring God's chastening that we make spiritual progress in our lives.

There is something about progress: it is much easier for it not to happen. The more you endure, the longer you endure, and the more difficult the trials and testings you endure, the greater will be the progress you make in your walk with the Lord and your work for the Lord. We must see the progressive benefits of enduring chastening. It is much slower to go forward for God than it is to go backward away from God. Picture the Christian life as climbing up a mountain. As long as we are ascending the mountain, our progress will be slow, but we are moving forward. If we fall, we start moving very rapidly—in the wrong direction.

I have known people who were faithful to God for many years. They followed Him, were active in church, were a blessing and encouragement to others, and were moving up the mountain. They were growing and maturing and drawing closer to God. Yet, in the space of just months or even days, they can undo all of the effort of those years. It is always faster to regress than it is to progress. Sometimes it is hard to realize that we are making any progress at all. Our growth seems so slow that we think we are standing still. But, we are never standing still—we are either moving forward or falling back. We are either moving up or moving down.

Hebrews Chapter 5 was written to speak to believers who were not growing as they should. Hebrews 5:12 uses the analogy of education, *"For when for the time ye ought to be teachers, ye have need that one teach you again which be the first principles of the oracles of God."* Now educationally, where do we get the first principles? We start learning the basics when we are in kindergarten. To these adult believers, he is saying, "You ought to have your graduate degree and be teaching others; and yet, here you are stuck in kindergarten." What an insult! They were not making progress. Why? Because they were not enduring chastening. In fact, in verse thirteen he calls them babies, and that is not a compliment. As long as I endure chastening, I am making progress, whether I can see it or not. Faith lets me believe progress is happening whether it feels like it or not.

The progress we are making in our spiritual life is not going to be measured in a day. It is not measured in weeks, months, or even a year. However, over a period of time, the progress *will* be measurable. We see that by faith. By the way, I have to see that in myself, and I have to see that in other people by faith. It can be very discouraging to work with people, to make sacrifices and investments, and have it feel like nothing is changing. When I see through the eyes of faith, I can endure the disappointments, and I can endure the chastening. As long as we endure chastening, we are going to make progress for the Lord.

Focus on Graduation – Take Advanced Classes

Second, **we must see afterward**. To have joy during chastening, we must see the temporary nature of our present dilemma. Afterward is coming. Not only are things not as they seem to be, they will also not be as they seem. No matter how tough the coursework in Adversity University gets, graduation day is coming. God has placed you where you are for a future purpose. When Joseph looked back on all the things that had happened to him—being sold into slavery by his own brothers, falsely accused and thrown in prison, and forgotten by those he had helped—he said, *"But as for you, ye thought evil against me; but God meant it unto good, to bring to pass, as it is this day, to save much people alive."* (Genesis 50:20)

In the future, as you move forward in your life, past the pressures and the difficulties and exams that you are taking right now, they are not going to seem nearly as difficult as they do today. That is because God is going to have "bigger fish for you to fry." He is going to have bigger challenges for you to experience. The classes keep getting tougher and tougher until the day He calls you home. Jesus is our pattern for looking to afterward. *"Who for the joy that was set before him, endured the cross."* (Hebrews 12:2) He did not focus on the cross; He focused on the crown. He knew He was on His way back home. He knew His work was almost finished. He knew that even amid the horrible pain and suffering, there was hope in the future. When you get to the point where you can look at afterward, you can laugh and smile and praise God, even in the midst of adversity. It will put a "spring in your step" and a "song in your heart." To have joy in adversity, we must see afterward.

It Will Be Worth It All

Third, **we must see the fruit.** The fruit of righteousness—of being like Jesus Christ—is (or at least should be) the goal of our lives. Righteousness is God's purpose in saving you (Romans 8:29), and it is produced by enduring chastening. If you do not have any interest in the fruit of righteousness, in being like Christ, then you need to examine your heart and see if you are truly God's child. Hebrews 12 makes it clear that there are people who think they are in the family who are not. Or, perhaps you have allowed bitterness during the chastening to blind you to what God is trying to accomplish through the adversity in your life. There is a tremendous peace that comes with the fruit of righteousness. There is the peace of being right with God and not fearing His judgment. There is peace in being right with yourself and not being condemned by your conscience. There is peace in being right with others and not worrying about those to whom you have done wrong.

In the heart of every child of God there should be a hatred for selfishness, for sin, for that which brings turmoil into our lives, and that which disappoints the Saviour. Yet, so often we love our sin and despise God's chastening. There is only sorrow and bitterness and pain in that life. But, we can see joy in the midst of God's chastening if we will see and love the fruit—the result that God has in mind in preparing your course work. Students who stick with Adversity University, maintain a good GPA, do the course work, go to class, and do not give up will receive a good report. But, they receive more than that; they also receive joy in the middle of their adversity and chastening. In a world filled with wrong, there is nothing that can compare to living with the peace-filled fruit of righteousness.

When I was a boy, our church supported the Shepherd's Home, a ministry for the mentally retarded in Union Grove, Wisconsin. Each year, Dr. Wood, the head of the ministry, would bring a group from the home to our church. Some years, they brought a hand bell group; other years, they brought a choir. Each time they came, those mentally challenged adults would perform music to glorify God. They would always close their presentation with the same singer. This man was obviously handicapped, but he had a beautiful voice. Many times, he would mess up a word or two, but there was a love for God in his heart that came through as he sang. I remember as a little boy listening to him sing:

> *Oft time our day seems long*
> *Our trials hard to bear,*
> *We're tempted to complain*
> *To murmur and despair,*
> *But Christ will soon appear*
> *To catch His bride away,*
> *All tears forever over*
> *In God's eternal day.*
> *It will be worth it all*

When we see Jesus,
Life's trials will seem so small
When we see Christ.
One glimpse of His dear face
All sorrows will erase,
So bravely run the race
Till we see Christ.

Ask God to help you see through the eyes of faith that your chastening will not endure forever; and that when it is finished, He will make us like God's Son.

16. PRACTICE MAKES PERFECT

"And ye hath forgotten the exhortation which speaketh unto you as unto children, My son despise not thou the chastening of the Lord, nor faint when thou art rebuked of Him: For whom the Lord loveth He chasteneth, and scourgeth every son whom He receiveth. If ye endure chastening, God dealeth with you as with sons; for what son is he whom the father chasteneth not? But if ye be without chastisement, whereof all are partakers, then are ye bastards, and not sons. Furthermore we have had fathers of our flesh which corrected us, and we gave them reverence: shall we not much rather be in subjection unto the Father of spirits, and live? For they verily for a few days chastened us after their own pleasure; but he for our profit, that we might be partakers of his holiness. Now no chastening for the present seemeth to be joyous, but grievous: nevertheless afterward it yieldeth the peaceable fruit of righteousness unto them which are exercised thereby;" —Hebrews 12:5-11

Being Conditioned

We looked at what allows us to have joy during chastening; now I want to call your attention to a very small phrase that makes a very big difference. We want the peaceable fruit of righteousness that comes from chastening, but it is not automatic. Every child of God is chastened, but not every child of God receives the benefit of chastening. The end of verse eleven tells us that the benefit comes to those *"which are exercised thereby."* The problem is that many of us are not willing to endure the practice required to become perfect. The world was amazed when Michael Phelps won eight gold medals at the Beijing Olympics. Many people would like gold medals—but not many people want to swim five hours or more every single day.

Custom-Designed Chastening

The word *"exercised"* comes from the Greek word *gymnazo*, from which we get the word gymnasium. It means to exercise vigorously with the idea of bringing about conditioning for future performance. It was used for an athlete putting in months and even years of preparation behind the scenes getting ready for their public performance. God's chastening in and of itself is does not produce the peaceable fruit of righteousness in our lives. That is only produced if we are motivated through the chastening to exercise, to intensely practice, that we might become better in that particular area or aspect of life that God is focusing on improving in us. Just as a trainer designs a specific exercise program to develop certain parts of the body, God custom designs our exercise program. All of His chastening is directed toward those specific areas of our lives and our character in which we are weak, in which we are undernourished, or in which we are not proficient.

God's chastening is custom designed for your area of need. For example, He wants you to be an excellent manager of His money. So God brings adversity into your life and finances to hone your skills. At that point, we have a choice to make. We can either exercise and develop our skills, or we can resist the chastening, complaining about how we always have money trouble. If you struggle with getting upset with people, God is going to bring people into your life that upset you more and more and more. Every course of study in Adversity University is individually custom-designed. The decision we make is how we respond. Do we allow the chastening to discourage us, or does it motivate us to look for ways to accomplish God's purpose and be strengthened through practice.

The word "habit" is a neutral word. There are good habits and bad habits. A habit is simply something that we have become accustomed to doing. Of course, it is much easier to develop bad habits; in fact, unless we exercise ourselves to develop good habits, it is automatic to develop bad habits! If we yield to our natural way of thinking, we end up with a natural way of living. To formulate a good habit, we have to "go against the current." God says, "I have placed chastening in your life, because I want you to become proficient in all these areas of life." That is how God brings us to a place of spiritual maturity. So, the cliché really is true: practice does make perfect. Those who practice with intensity receive the benefit of God's chastening. To better understand this concept of *exercise*, let's look at some other places in Scripture where it appears.

Exercise our Minds

First, **we need to exercise our minds**. First Timothy 4:7-8 says, *"But refuse profane and old wives' fables, and exercise thyself rather unto godliness. For bodily exercise profiteth little: but godliness is profitable unto all things, having promise of the life that now is, and of that which is to come."* The context of these verses is talking about our way of thinking. To know true godliness, we must refuse philosophies, ideas, and ways of thinking that are opposed to God's truth. Paul calls them "profane," meaning not filled with cursing, but rather common and unholy. We must learn to distinguish between truth and lies. If you will exercise yourself unto that end, then you will become a godly individual. What we think in our minds directs our actions. God chastens us in the area of our thinking. Nobody thinks rightly just by getting up one morning and saying, "You know what? I am going to become a right thinker." You have to exercise your mind to think rightly because you are naturally going to think wrong. Our natural thoughts are carnal and selfish. That is innate within us, and God chastens us to change our thinking from the natural to the supernatural.

First Timothy chapter four gives us some specific examples of areas where we need to think God's way instead of our way. Verse one talks about people who depart from the faith because they give heed (pay attention) to the false teachings of devils. The best way to evaluate any idea or doctrine—in fact the only reliable way—is by comparing it to what the Bible says. You should be able to base everything you believe on the Scriptures. Otherwise, you do not have a solid foundation for your faith. Timothy was instructed to remind the people he pastored of the truth. *"If thou put the brethren in remembrance of these things, thou shalt be a good minister of Jesus Christ, nourished up in the words of faith."* (I Timothy 4:6) It is pitiful to see immature believers who have been saved for many years still stuck in kindergarten. They need to exercise their minds and grow up.

Exercise our Senses

Second, **we must exercise our senses.** Hebrews 5:14 says, *"But strong meat belongeth to them that are of full age, even those who by reason of use have their senses exercised to discern both good and evil."* God wants us to exercise our senses that we might discern between that which is good and that which is evil. Now what are our senses? We have five senses: hearing, seeing, tasting, touching, and smelling. All the information that comes into the three pound computer we call the brain comes in through those senses, naturally speaking. When you were a baby, you did not know what was good and what was bad. If your parents put good food in your mouth, you might spit it out. Over time, you learn as you are disciplined, corrected, and instructed. The same process must be taking place in our spiritual lives as well.

Immature Christians make bad decisions because their spiritual senses cannot distinguish between right and wrong. Everything we take into our minds will affect the way we think; therefore, we need to be weighing and measuring it. What we hear needs to be disciplined. Is it helpful; is it uplifting; will it help me mature? If not, why am I putting it into my brain? If we just open our ears and listen to everything and everyone without discernment, then we will never grow. The exercising of my senses also involves practicing observation—what we see. If I do not discipline my eyes to look away from that which is evil, then I will grow accustomed to it over time. Lot first pitched his tent toward (facing) Sodom. After he got used to how it looked, he moved in. The devil does not try to pull you all the way off course at once; he is very happy with small steps in the wrong direction.

Recently, I was counseling someone who had gotten caught up in horrible, destructive viewing habits. This was someone who should have known better. He said to me, "Brother Kingsbury, it just started with one brief view at an internet site. Now, I cannot stop." The discipline of what we see, what we listen to, what we touch; the discipline of our senses is an exercise that must be practiced if we are going to mature and develop as men and women of God. The natural man, a person who is without Christ, can only rely on the five senses that they have. When a person gets born again though, they have a sixth sense, a spiritual sense; the indwelling of the Spirit of God. That indwelling happens at the moment of salvation, but that does not mean that the new believer is in tune with that spiritual sense. You must learn to habitually listen to the Spirit of God. The more you say "Yes" to Him, the better you become at listening to Him.

I have heard people say, "Well, I do not know what to do. I wish God would speak to me." Are you doing what He has spoken to you about already? If not, why would He speak further? But, if you are willing to do what He has spoken to you about already, He will start speaking to you. God knows our hearts. He knows whether we are willing or not. We can sing "All to Jesus I Surrender" until the cows come home, but that does not make it true. It takes discipline and practice to learn to habitually listen to the voice of the Spirit. The first time I yielded to the Spirit, I was amazed at how loudly He began talking to me. That is because He knew I was listening. To exercise our senses, we have to habitually listen, look at, eat, touch, and smell that which helps us grow spiritually.

Exercise Unselfish Generosity

Third, **we must not exercise covetousness.** Second Peter 2:14 says, *"Having eyes full of adultery, and that cannot cease from sin; beguiling unstable souls: an heart they have exercised with covetous practices; cursed children."* It is true that practice makes perfect; but it is true both positively and negatively. Just as we can develop strong spiritual muscles through exercise, we can develop strong tendencies to evil. Peter here is talking about people whose innate covetousness and selfishness has been developed and strengthened. That have taken the natural human tendency to focus on "me first" and made it habitual.

In reality, what they are doing is becoming strong to sin. That is a very dangerous way for a child of God to live.

The example Peter uses of this truth is that of Balaam. Balaam knew the truth, and he was respected as a man who could speak for God. But, he had a flaw—he was willing to sell out his convictions and the truth for money. Balaam habitually made decisions on the basis of, "How will this line my pockets? How will this benefit me?" It ended up costing Balaam his life. He was killed along with the enemies of God. How do you overcome covetousness? You overcome it by practicing unselfish generosity. God's chastening in our lives will bring about spiritual maturity if we are motivated to exercise and put into practice habits that lead to clear, Scriptural thinking. That leads to spiritual sensitivity and control of our senses. If we gain a pure heart through unselfish generosity, we then can become mature children of God.

The Product of Exercise

A lot of churches are knocking themselves out to try to entertain their kids. Our philosophy that we have strongly ingrained in our church for our young people is that it is not about a lot of games and things like that, but it is about our young people being servants. I have had people ask, "Why is that so important?" It is important because we are trying to build good habits now, so that when they are older and temptation comes, they can resist it. If they get habitually used to doing that which is good and right and unselfish, it is difficult to break that and get them to do wrong. We are trying to build patterns of behavior that will last for the rest of their lives.

My wife's cousin, Donna, and her husband, Jim, are dear friends of ours. When we were dating, we were not allowed to date alone; so the four of us double-dated. When their daughter, Angie, and her husband, Chris, decided to go the mission field in New Guinea, I was not surprised at all. They are ministering way out in the back country. The living conditions are primitive. They are making huge sacrifices to be there and to bring the gospel to those people. Why am I not surprised that they are willing to give up so much for others? Years ago, we were in Kalamazoo, Michigan, visiting family for Christmas where I grew up. We drove by the Kalamazoo Rescue Mission, where I preached my very first sermon and there were Jim, Donna, and their girls, served Christmas dinner to the men. You do not just wake up one day and decide to be unselfish and sacrificial. It is the product of exercise. Angie is on the mission field because she learned, at a young age, to live for others. Start building the habits for the life that you know God wants you to live as a mature believer today, by exercising...the rewards will be worth it!

17. God's Workout Program – Strengthening the Hands

"Now no chastening for the present seemeth to be joyous, but grievous: nevertheless afterward it yieldeth the peaceable fruit of righteousness unto them which are exercised thereby. Wherefore lift up the hands which hang down, and the feeble knees; And make straight paths for your feet, lest that which is lame be turned out of the way; but let it rather be healed." —Hebrews 12:11-13

Custom-Designed Curriculum

A year ago, I found out what happens when you have a heart attack. Oh, I have known a lot of people who had heart attacks. I have been to hospitals to pray with and for them. I have read about all the symptoms, but it is different when you feel them. Before they released me from the hospital, they gave me a custom-designed workout program to improve my cardiovascular strength and help prevent another heart attack. I told you that God designs the curriculum in Adversity University specifically for each believer, and this was the same way. It was planned just for me. My cardio regimen was not a pleasant program. It was rigorous. I did not get up in the morning and say, "I can't wait to get down to the gym and get on that elliptical trainer!" I would get used to one level on the treadmill, and then they would make it go faster and increase the angle so it was higher and create more resistance to make me work harder. I hated that program, but I knew that it was for my benefit.

In the last chapter, we talked about the importance of exercise and what we should exercise; now we are going to look at the workout program God has designed for us. When I was in junior high school, gym class was non-optional. My teacher was Mr. Santangilo, and he delighted in making us do leg lifts. That was the exercise I despised the most. We had to lie flat on the floor in the gym with our legs together and lift our feet. It would not have been as bad if he had let us do full leg lifts, bringing our legs all the way up, but he insisted we hold our legs about six inches off the ground. Mr. Santangilo would say, "One!" That meant we had to lift our legs off the ground. Then he would come around and watch our feet and the way we were holding our legs. I remember saying in my heart, "Please, say two." When he said "Two," we would spread our legs apart and keep holding them about six inches above the ground. Then, on "Three," we brought the legs back together again. The muscles were tense, and the legs were sore, and I thought he never would say, "Four," which is when we could put them down. He sure counted slowly!

Non-Optional Classes

Then we would do it all over again...and again...and again. I hated gym class. But it was not optional—I could not quit. A guy could try not doing the exercises, but Mr. Santangilo had a motivational device in his office called a paddle. So, we did the leg lifts, and the jumping jacks, and the push ups, and the sit ups, and ran laps just like he told us to do. God has assigned us non-optional chastening, because He loves us so much. He brings adversity, pressures, problems and people into our lives as part of His custom workout program prepared just for us.

And we get to make a choice: we can both participate in the program and experience the pain of the workout, or we can try to avoid the program and experience the pain of it anyway. Notice that there is no way to avoid pain; it is coming either way. The question is whether we will benefit from it or suffer from it. Let's look at God's exercise program, and what it is designed to do in our lives.

Exercise Your Hands for Work

First, **God's workout program is designed to strengthen our hands for work**. The hands mentioned in verse twelve are a metaphor for our work for the Lord. So, God has designed our training to make us stronger in His work. More than fifty times, the Bible talks about the work of a man's or woman's hands. Work is not a curse; it is a blessing. Adam had work assignments even before the "Fall." There is a work that God has called every one of us to do. Too many people think that God's calling is restricted to preachers and missionaries. If you are doing the work God has called you to do, it is sacred work, whether you are a pastor or a plumber; a missionary or a machinist. For the children of God, there is such thing as sacred and secular; everything we do is to be done "as to the Lord." (Colossians 3:23) Wherever you work, you are working for the Lord. No obedient Christian serves God part-time.

Verse twelve talks about hands that are hanging down. Remember the story of the battle the Israelites fought in the wilderness. As long as Moses held his hands up, the Israelites were winning; when he got tired and his hands fell, the Israelites started losing. Aaron and Hur held up Moses' arms so Israel could win the battle. (Exodus 17:8-13) God wants our hands to be strengthened, so that our capacity for work is increased. He does not want us to fail in the work or in the battle. Over and over again, the Bible talks about the importance of work.

"And that ye study to be quiet, and to do your own business, and to work with your own hands, as we commanded you." (1 Thessalonians 4:11)

"Not slothful in business, fervent in spirit, serving the Lord." (Romans 12:11)

"And labor, working with our own hands: being reviled, we bless; being persecuted, we suffer it." (1 Corinthians 4:12)

"Let him that stole steal no more; but rather let him labour, working with his hands the thing which is good, that he may have to give to him that needeth." (Ephesians 4:28)

The strength of our hands, our capacity to be productive, our capacity to work, our capacity to carry burdens in the work that God has called us to do, will never increase unless the intensity of our exercise increases. If you go to the gym to work out and only lift the barbell without putting weights on it, then you are not going to get any stronger. God is not going to let you stay there. He is going to add more weight. He is going to compel you to lift up your hands. God is not doing that to punish us; He is doing it to increase our capacity to be productive.

Joseph is a great illustration of this truth. He was a sheep herder. If God had not stretched him, he would have stayed a sheep herder. God wanted him to lead a great nation, but he was not ready. He had to go through trials and tribulations and struggles to increase his strength. God allowed Joseph to be sold as a slave. God allowed him to be falsely accused of rape. God allowed him to be forgotten in the prison. At every step along the way, Joseph was learning skills and strengthening his faith, so that he would be stronger for the work God had for him to do. Most of us would be happy to run a country. We would like the power and prestige that comes with the position. But, most of us do not want to go through what Joseph went through to be strengthened to handle the responsibilities. And God will not give responsibilities like that to people who cannot handle them.

You are in a workout program today. God sees your potential.

He has a calling and a destination for your life. He will not bring you there automatically, and He will not bring you there without adversity. You will not arrive there until you cooperate with Him and accept the difficult assignments that will prepare you to lift up your hands to the work that God has called you to do. Someone said, "Do not pray for lighter loads; pray for stronger arms." It is through increased strength, that we become better husbands, better wives, better parents, better grandpas and grandmas, better laborers, become better bosses, better teachers and preachers and bus workers. All the adversity and pressures and problems that are part of your daily life are from God to strengthen you so that you can lift up your hands, and so you can do more for Him. No one does great things for God without experiencing great adversity.

Exercise Your Hands for Prayer

Second, **God's workout program is designed to strengthen our hands for prayer.** In 1 Timothy 2:8, Paul wrote, *"I will therefore that men pray everywhere, lifting up holy hands, without wrath and doubting."* What does that mean? In the Hebrew culture, it was common for people to raise their hands up toward Heaven while they prayed; in fact, many Jewish people still do that today. Psalm 28:2 says, *"Hear the voice of my supplications, when I cry unto thee, when I lift up my hands toward thy holy oracle."* God intensifies the burdens and pressures in my life, so that I will develop as a man of prayer.

I remember when our children were young. When they needed help, they would stretch their little hands up into the air, wanting us to reach down and help them. I think sometimes God looks down from Heaven at us and says, "Why are you bearing that burden yourself? Just lift up your hands and ask Me for help." As long as I can handle whatever I am facing by myself, I do not need to lift up my hands. So to strengthen me for prayer, God says, "I'm going to send you to the gym, Paul. I've got a workout program designed to improve your prayer life." Again, we face a choice. I have seen people who were faced with adversity shake their fist in God's face and say, "How can you do this to me?" I have seen others lift up their hands in desperation and say, "Oh God, I need Your help. I'm crying out to You."

Daniel was a great man of prayer. He had an unshakable habit of praying three times every day. Now, these were not just "bless this food" mealtime prayers; they were serious, sustained seasons of prayer when Daniel was talking to God. Why did Daniel pray so much? He had to! Imagine being taken from your home when you were a teenager and being placed in an indoctrination program in a heathen country specifically designed to turn you away from your God. Imagine being forced to stand up for what is right when almost no one else did. Of course Daniel prayed! When Nebuchadnezzar threatened to kill all the wise men (including Daniel) unless someone could tell him what his dream had been, Daniel and the three Hebrew children spent all night praying instead of sleeping. In the morning, God gave Daniel the answer. Decades passed, and Daniel was still praying. He spent a night in a den of lions because he would not stop praying.

Daniel chapter ten tells us that even when he was an old man (probably at least in his 80's), God stirred up his prayer life again. The amazing revelation of the future that God gave to Daniel only came after he fasted and prayed, not for a day or two, but for twenty-one days! Daniel could not have handled that when he was a teenager. That burden would have been too heavy for him then. But, over the years (through adversity, hardship, struggle, and crisis), Daniel's hands were strengthened in prayer. God may give you a burden that is heavier than you think you can bear, but He will never give you a burden that He will not help you carry—if you lift up your hands to Him in prayer. But, do not make the mistake of thinking this process is going to stop. If you can lift this burden to Him, then next month or next year, He will give you a burden that exceeds it. You are going to have to lift up your hands to Him again.

A Personal Exercise

Since my birth in 1953 until the birth of our handicapped daughter in 1988, I never had to ask God for money. I had worked and received income since I was twelve years old; I had tithed faithfully, and spent somewhat carefully. As an adult, the church I pastored generously cared for our needs. However, God had a course for me in faith (and economics) when the cap of one million dollars was reached on our health insurance policy as a result of our daughter's extreme health needs. As a result, we (me, my wife, and our children) were compelled to turn to God for help with a financial need.

I received a medical bill for two thousand dollars informing me that our insurance had run out. That very week, my wife and I were scheduled to go out of town for a brief holiday gifted to us by a generous friend of the family. We told our children at family devotions of the need and asked them to pray, committing this to the Lord with the promise NOT to tell anyone that the preacher needed two thousand dollars for his daughter's medical needs.

The following Sunday evening, while vacationing, I spoke with our assistant pastor, and he told me of the events of the day. I was surprised as he told me that there had been an anonymous gift of two thousand dollars given in the offering to our family. Now, I was very happy; however, I doubted that our children had kept quiet about our need. I just knew that one of them had said *something* to *someone* while attending our Christian school. Upon our return home, I received the promised check. I gathered, once again, with our family, and I asked them if they had prayed for the money. They all said that indeed they had requested that God would give us two thousand dollars. "Did any of you tell anyone about this need?" I enquired. None of them had, and I could tell that they were sincere. Then, I took the check out of my pocket and held it up for them to see. Imagine their joy as they rejoiced with their mother and me at God's miraculous provision.

Jason, our oldest son, was particularly impressed with this answer to prayer. He said, "Dad, I have read the stories of answered prayer in the Bible, and it really didn't mean much to me; but now that God has answered my prayer, I now know that I serve an awesome God!

Exercise Your Hands for Praise

Third, **God's workout program is designed to strengthen our hands for praise**. Psalm 63:4 says, "*Thus will I bless thee while I live: I will lift up my hands in thy name.*" Psalm 134:2 says, "*Lift up your hands in the sanctuary, and bless the Lord.*" One of the main purposes for which we were created is to give praise to God. It is easy to praise Him when you are on top of the mountain. It is easy to lift up your hands in praise when you have experienced a great blessing, but what about in the hours of discouragement? What do you do in those times when those burdens are so heavy? That is when God develops our strength of praise. He says, "Now, I want you to lift up your hands unto Me. Now, I want to hear your praise."

Think of Job. In a single day, he lost everything—his possessions, his servants, and his children. "*Then Job arose, and rent his mantle, and shaved his head, and fell down upon the ground, and worshiped, And said, Naked came I out of my mother's womb, and naked shall I return thither: the Lord gave, and the Lord hath taken away; blessed be the name of the Lord."* (Job 1:20-21) Was it easy for Job to praise God when everything had gone wrong? No, of course not. But, over the years, he had strengthened his hands of praise. Praise may be difficult, but it is when we praise God sincerely in the midst of pain, that He is most glorified. He knows then that we are demonstrating Biblical faith; not rejoicing in the present circumstances; but in the reality, that He is using them to develop our strength.

Hebrews 13:15 says, *"By him therefore let us offer the sacrifice of praise to God continually, that is, the fruit of our lips giving thanks to his name."* Why is praise called a sacrifice? It is because truly praising God is not done on the basis of your circumstances or how things appear to be or how they feel, but praise is given because you know it is the right thing to do. Praise Him in difficult times, because you know that God does not make any mistakes. You can praise Him in the midst of pain, knowing that it will glorify His Name, and that He will be pleased, and that you will grow spiritually. Humanly speaking, this is absolutely impossible. But, notice that God does not ask us to praise Him in adversity on our own. How do we offer that sacrifice? *"By him."* He gives us the strength we need to sincerely praise the Lord when we hurt, when we feel like quitting or when the burdens are so heavy that we think that we cannot go on.

God puts us in His workout program to strengthen our hands for work, for prayer, and for praise. In the next chapter, we will look at the other two areas God's program for us is designed to strengthen and build.

18. GOD'S WORKOUT PROGRAM – STRENGTHENING THE FEEBLE KNEES

"Now no chastening for the present seemeth to be joyous, but grievous: nevertheless afterward it yieldeth the peaceable fruit of righteousness unto them which are exercised thereby. Wherefore lift up the hands which hang down, and the feeble knees; And make straight paths for your feet, lest that which is lame be turned out of the way; but let it rather be healed." –Hebrews 12:11-13

Imperative for Running the Race

God's exercise program, as we saw in the last chapter includes a plan to strengthen our hands. His education and His discipling include everyone and everything that impacts our lives as children of God. Having worked on our hands first, we see in verse twelve, that God is going to develop our knees. What exactly is a feeble-kneed person? Literally, a feeble-kneed person is one who is paralyzed. Luke 5:18 says, *"And behold, men brought in a bed a man which was taken with a palsy: and they sought means to bring him in and to lay him before him."* This is the story of the four men who brought their friend to Jesus and had to take the roof off the house to let him down that he might be healed. The Bible says he needed healing because he was sick of a palsy—the same word that is used here for feeble knees. A person with palsy is paralyzed; their legs are stiff and locked, so that they do not work properly.

Remember that Hebrews 12 starts off with the metaphor of the Christian life as a race. If your legs do not work, then you cannot run the race. If the enemy can lock your knees in place, then you will become paralyzed and have to stop running. So, God has an exercise program designed to loosen up your legs. This idea of paralyzed legs is found in several places in Scripture, and looking at them will help us see and understand God's exercise program for our legs. First, let's look at the life of Job.

"Then Eliphaz the Temanite answered and said, If we assay to commune with thee, wilt thou be grieved? but who can withhold himself from speaking? Behold, thou hast instructed many, and thou hast strengthened the weak hands. Thy words have upholden him that was falling, and thou hast strengthened the feeble knees. But now it is come upon thee, and thou faintest; it toucheth thee, and thou art troubled. Is not this thy fear, thy confidence, thy hope, and the uprightness of thy ways?" (Job 4:1-6)

Job was the example God picked from all of the people on earth to present as an example to Satan. He was a wise, mature believer of whom the Bible describes as a perfect, or complete, man. He is a great pattern for us to emulate. After Satan was given permission to attack Job, Job lost everything—his possessions, his children, and his health. Job's friends came to comfort him, although they ended up not doing a very good job at it! Here in Job 4, we see Eliphaz, one of Job's friends, talking. He says that once Job had strengthened the feeble knees of others, but now his own legs had become paralyzed. Why? What happened to this great Christian? Eliphaz tells us that Job's legs were paralyzed because of fear. And Job confirms that diagnosis. In Job 3:25-26 he said, *"For the thing which I greatly feared is come upon me, and that which I was afraid of is come unto me. I was not in safety, neither had I rest, neither was I quiet; yet trouble came."*

Fear Brings Paralysis

Notice that Job, even though he was a mature, godly Christian, was not exempt from falling prey to fear. Job's fear paralyzed his knees. The fear of what might happen can grip us strongly, even though it is not based on reality.

Job worried about his children (Job 1:15), and he worried about his wealth. I believe that there was a sense in which Job had come to trust his possessions rather than the God Who gave them. God removed everything from Job except Himself. When everything was gone, there was nothing left to be afraid of losing.

Though Job was the best Christian in the world, he still needed to completely rely on God. When we are paralyzed by fear, we open a door for the adversary to come in. And often, God in His providence will allow our worst fears to occur. This is not because He is angry at us, but it is because He wants us to see how foolish it is to live our lives paralyzed by what might take place. Job eventually came out of this affliction and did quite well. But, his knees had to be strengthened first. God strengthens your ability to overcome fear by having you face the fear.

Facing the Fear

Courage begets courage. Think of the story of David facing Goliath. Everyone else in the Israelite army was afraid, even King Saul who was the tallest man in the kingdom. When David got there, he was ready to take on the giant as soon as he heard what was going on. Why was David brave when no one else was? It is because while he was tending sheep, he had already faced his fear by killing a bear and a lion that attacked his lambs. God built David's courage little by little, so that when the "giant challenge" came, he was prepared. God is going to put you through adversity to overcome your fears and strengthen your knees.

Joe Clapp is our nephew. Joe lived with our family, along with his brothers and sister, following the death of their father to cancer in 1996 and mother in 1998. As an older teen, Joey (as he is affectionately known) was diagnosed with leukemia, which could only be reversed with a bone marrow transplant. Joey had enrolled in Bible college for the fall, but God placed him in Adversity University and his custom-designed class was an advanced course in faith. The Children's Hospital in Memphis, Tennessee, became his home for several months of intense pain and suffering through which his faith grew as he faced the inevitable fear of cancer. Having observed the consequences of his parent's similar illnesses, he knew that this trial of his faith would be exceptionally difficult. And it was.

With courage from God and generous support from family and friends, he faced the fear with unusual maturity, having been prepared for this trial by the experience of his parents' death. As a result, Joey passed his course and is serving God today.

Refusing to face fear with faith in God is catastrophic. Consider, for example, the people of God in the days of Ezekiel the prophet. *But they that escape of them shall escape, and shall be on the mountains like doves of the valleys, all of them mourning, every one for his iniquity. All hands shall be feeble, and all knees shall be weak as water. They shall also gird themselves with sackcloth, and horror shall cover them; and shame shall be upon all faces, and baldness upon all their heads. They shall cast their silver in the streets, and their gold shall be removed: their silver and their gold shall not be able to deliver them in the day of the wrath of the Lord: they shall not satisfy their souls, neither fill their bowels: because it is the stumbling block of their iniquity.* (Ezekiel 7:16-19)

Ezekiel ministered to the Jews at a low point in their spiritual lives. In the entire book of Ezekiel, there is not a single instance of anyone repenting and getting right with God, though Ezekiel preached to them with fervency. His wife died, and God told him not to even take one day off for mourning; just keep on preaching. All of the prophets had it rough, but Ezekiel may have had the toughest life of all. Here, in Ezekiel chapter 7, he described the backslidden believers who were running from God as being "weak-kneed." The people of God had chosen to defy God and His rules and His ways and His plan for their lives. As a result, God in His great love and compassion and justice brought down chastening upon His people. Because they still refused to repent, God took away the strength of their knees.

Triumph Over Fear

The expression "knees shall be weak as water" means they had no stability. God put a stumbling block in front of them to stop them from running. God will not allow His children to go on arrogantly and securely in their sin. If you are living away from the will of God, and you know it; and yet you are secure and feel safe and are having fun, it means one of two things; either you have not been gone very long, or you are not saved. God will bring fear into your life, a phobia that will bring you down on your face before Him just like someone who trips over a stumbling block. He does this, so that we will return to Him. In Christ, you find safety; in Christ, you find security; and in Christ, you find stability for your life once again. *"The way of the transgressor is hard."* (Proverbs 13:15) *"The wages of sin is death."* (Romans 6:23) That is not true only for the unconverted. Sin brings death. That is the ultimate result of fleeing the will of God for your life. The final example comes from the book of Isaiah.

The wilderness and the solitary place shall be glad for them; and the desert shall rejoice, and blossom as the rose. It shall blossom abundantly, and rejoice even with joy and singing: the glory of Lebanon shall be given unto it, the excellency of Carmel and Sharon, they shall see the glory of the Lord, and the excellency of our God. Strengthen ye the weak hands, and confirm the feeble knees. Say to them that are of a fearful heart, Be strong, fear not: behold, your God will come with vengeance, even God with a recompence; he will come and save you. (Isaiah 35:1-4)

This is a prophetic passage that is primarily speaking about a time that is still in the future. Israel has returned to the Promised Land as a nation, but they have not yet turned back to God. During the Tribulation period, there will 144,000 Jewish missionaries who will travel and preach that Jesus is the Messiah. They will suffer great hardship and persecution; yet Isaiah is telling them to be strong and trust in God. Notice that even after we return to the Lord and are walking in obedience to His will, there are still times when we can become afraid.

God is reminding us that even when the world seems to be crashing down around us, we can trust God to keep His promise to deliver us. Even though the world is filled with evil, troubles, and fears, God will keep His children. And, we have so much to look forward to in the future.

One day, the Rose of Sharon, the Lily of the Valley, the Bright and Morning Star, our Savior, the Lord Jesus Christ will rule and reign, not only over Jerusalem, not only over the nation of Israel, but over all of the earth. And, we who have decided to follow Jesus, we who have decided to answer the clarion call of the gospel, we who have decided to enter the race and run with patience, we who have decided to overcome our fear, we will triumph, and we will win. We must simply hope in God, because He will save us. You do not have to be afraid. God does not want you to be paralyzed. If you are paralyzed with fear, it may be because God is dealing with your fear of what has not happed yet. It may be because you have been living in disobedience to God and are trying to run away from Him. Or, it may be that even though you are right with the Lord, you still find yourself afraid. Whatever the case, you need to respond properly. If fear besets you, trust in God. If you know you are disobedient, repent, and run back to Him. If you are surrounded by fears while following Him, trust in His Word, and He will save you. Dealing with fear will strengthen your legs for the race. So, having dealt with the hands and the legs, let's move on and see how God works on our feet.

19. God's Workout Program – Strengthening the Feet

"Now no chastening for the present seemeth to be joyous, but grievous: nevertheless afterward it yieldeth the peaceable fruit of righteousness unto them which are exercised thereby. Wherefore lift up the hands which hang down, and the feeble knees; And make straight paths for your feet, lest that which is lame be turned out of the way; but let it rather be healed." –Hebrews 12:11-13

Clear the Path

The final part of God's gym program for you is to prepare your feet for the race. To do that, He says we need straight paths for our feet. The Greek word translated straight is *orthos*—from which we get the word *orthopedics*. When the Bible says, "make straight paths for your feet" it is literally talking about clearing away obstacles and smoothing out of the pathway of its bumps and potholes, so the runner has a smooth track on which to run. So many times, we look at the things that are happening and wonder, "God, what are You doing here?" God is training us to be straight. He is motivating me to clear the obstacles out of the pathway, so I can maximize the ability He has given to me to run the race with endurance.

The picture here is of athletes who have been trained to run in the races. They have a prescribed course that they're going to run. So prior to running the race, they go along the course and they clear out the weeds that have grown up. They take the stumps and remove them, and then fill in the holes that have developed in the path. All this work is done in order that when they run the race, they minimize the potential of stumbling, of twisting or breaking an ankle and injuring themselves. All of the training, all of the gym work, all of the exercise, and all of the preparation would not pay off if they tripped and fell on the course. All of the adversity and trouble from God that has influenced my life is designed to motivate me, to challenge me, to pressure or compel me, and to remove any obstacle that stands in the way of my ability to run the Christian race. This is essential in determining the success or failure in your life in running the race for God.

God wants you to be successful in running the race; the course of life that He has for you. It is natural that there will be obstacles in the way. It is natural that there will be potholes and ridges in the road. So He wants you to spend time to remove the obstacles that would hinder you from successfully running the race. Earlier, we talked about removing the weight and the sin which doth so easily beset us personally. This particular cleanup is talking about the area around us – the atmosphere in which we live and move and have our being. You see, it is very, very important for the successful running of the Christian race, that you and I be conscious of the influences we allow within our sphere of influence. Our lives must be free of the encumbrances of those things or those people that could cause us to stumble and fall.

Primary Obstacle

I have been in the ministry a long time, and my observation is that the number one reason people drop out of the Christian race is other people. If you set out to do the will of God and be a runner in the race, you cannot afford to surround yourself with worldly, discouraging people, or old friends who will pull you back. If you do, they will trip you up. My son-in-law told me this true story. There was a young man at the Bible college he went to who was a gifted preacher. I got to hear him preach once, and it was obvious that he had the power of God on his life. Matt said, "You know, Dad, he doesn't even go to church anymore. He's quit on God and just forsaken the faith." I asked, "What in the world happened?" It turned out that the young preacher had committed huge amounts of Scripture to memory. He kept all the verses he had memorized on cards in a leather attaché case, and another student stole it. It made him so mad and bitter, that he no longer goes to church at all! That was an obstacle that he tripped over. Who do you think planted that obstacle? Who do you think wanted him to trip up? The devil did. The obstacles are not to be tripped over; they are to be removed.

Not only do we remove obstacles to ensure we can keep running, but we also remove them to maintain a helpful testimony. We see this in the expression "lest that which is lame be turned out of the way." A lame person is someone who has been hurt. As we run the race, we are not running alone. We talked earlier about the cloud of witnesses in Heaven; but we are also being watched by other runners here on earth. How we respond to the obstacles we face is going to have a direct impact on those people. Those people who have been hurt, those who have bruises and sprains have not quit running yet; but if they see us fall, they may drop out of the race. What does it mean to be turned out of the way? It means to stop following the path that God has laid out for your race.

For the Sake of Others

It is not enough just to avoid tripping over the obstacles; we need to remove them. An obstacle that I can easily clear as a mature believer might be a stumbling block to a young Christian. I do not just remove the obstacle for my own sake, but I remove it for the sake of others. That is why it is not good for us to try to live our lives on the edge. "Is there a specific verse that directly says I cannot do that?" is the wrong question. The right question is, "Is this the best?" There is far more to the race than just right and wrong; remember that there are weights as well as sins that we need to lay aside. You can say that you are a strong enough Christian to handle it, and that may be true (although it is dangerous to think so), but that does not mean it will not hurt someone else. Do not turn someone who has been wounded out of the way.

The concept of straight paths was also the theme of the ministry of John the Baptist. In fact, it shows up in all four Gospel records of his preaching. You can find it in Matthew 3, Mark 1, Luke 3, and John 1. John's ministry was foretold by the prophet Isaiah. Look at this account from Luke.

"And he came into all the country about Jordan, preaching the baptism of repentance for the remission of sins; As it is written in the book of the words of Esaias the prophet, saying, The voice of one crying in the wilderness, Prepare ye the way of the Lord, make his paths straight. Every valley shall be filled, and every mountain and hill shall be brought low; and the crooked shall be made straight, and the rough ways shall be made smooth; And all flesh shall see the salvation of God. Then said he to the multitude that came forth to be baptized of him, O generation of vipers, who hath warned you to flee from the wrath to come? Bring forth therefore fruits worthy of repentance, and begin not to say within yourselves, We have Abraham to our father: for I say unto you, That God is able of these stones to raise up children unto Abraham. And now also the axe is laid unto the root of the trees: every tree therefore which bringeth not forth good fruit is hewn down, and cast into the fire." (Luke 3:3-9)

John did not pull any punches when he preached. Eventually, he got his head cut off because he preached so pointedly and hard against sin. He reproved Herod for taking his brother's wife; and Herod's wife was so offended, she schemed to get John killed. What is the application that God would have us draw from the testimony of John the Baptist? A straight path is sure evidence of genuine repentance. John said to his audience, "Listen, you say you believe in God. Well, fine, if you are a genuine believer, then it is going to be demonstrated by your behavior." The people were not used to that. They did not mind acknowledging a belief, but John was demanding action to match. John told them to bring forth fruits that were evidence of the repentance they claimed. If we take seriously the issue of clearing our path of those things that hinder us and others, it demonstrates what we really believe.

Path Demonstrates Belief

Every time there is a problem with behavior, there is a problem with belief. John's message was that the Messiah was coming, and people needed to get ready. Make the path straight; clear out all that junk that is in your life; clear your home; clear your mind; and clear your personal life. In our day in the 21st century, the kind of preaching John the Baptist did is still not accepted. Most of what comes forth from pulpits is nothing more than sweet, syrupy pabulum that is being fed to people to try to make them feel good about themselves. You can get a crowd that way and make lots of money. That is what people want; but it is not what they need. The ministry is not about seeing how much money you can get and how big of a crowd you can draw. It is about honoring and glorifying God.

You say, "Well, why would anybody do that?" They do it so they are able to pay their bills, that's why! They do it to get more people in. After all, isn't that what it's all about, seeing how much money you can get and how many people you can get in? No, that is not what it is all about. It is about honoring and glorifying God.

Path of Holiness

Isaiah used the analogy of the path eight times. You know what he called the path? God told him to call this path, the path of holiness. John the Baptist was the fulfillment of the prophecy, but I want to call you attention to the emphasis Isaiah put on our conduct.

Comfort ye, comfort ye my people, saith your God. Speak ye comfortable to Jerusalem, and cry unto her, that her warfare is accomplished, that her iniquity is pardoned: for she hath received of the Lord's hand double for all her sins. The voice of him that crieth in the wilderness, Prepare ye the way of the Lord, make straight in the desert a highway for our God. Every valley shall be exalted, and every mountain and hill shall be made low: and the crooked shall be made straight, and the rough places plain: And the glory of the Lord shall be revealed, and all flesh shall see it together: for the mouth of the Lord hath spoken it." (Isaiah 40:1-5)

The first century believer who reads Hebrews would have stopped at this passage to consider the encouragement of Isaiah's prophetical promise to the people of God. It would have been very familiar to them. They understood that in the days of ancient kingdoms, before a king would go out and visit his subjects, he would send heralds. These men would go ahead of the king along a prescribed path to announce his coming. And before the king would come, the people were expected to make sure the road was fit for a king. They would straighten and smooth the road as much as they could. They would remove trash and debris from the sides of the road. They would fill in the potholes and try to make sure the path was straight and ready.

So God's workout program for our feet involves: clearing the path as runners in the race, making sure our lives reflect true repentance, and preparing for the coming of the King. This is exercise, physical struggle, and hard work. I wish there was a way to run the race without all the effort, but there is not. Stay in the gym. Keep working out. Do not skip your training. And, if you do those things, you will be a champion in running the race.

20. THE HIGH COST OF DROPPING OUT

"Looking diligently let any man fail of the grace of God; lest any root of bitterness springing up trouble you, and thereby many be defiled; Lest there be any fornicator, or profane person, as Esau, who for one morsel of meat sold his birthright. For ye know how that afterward, when he would have inherited the blessing, he was rejected: for he found no place of repentance, though he sought it carefully with tears." —Hebrews 12:15-17

Be Cautioned

Have I convinced you yet that the race is hard? I am sure you did not need me to tell you that! We have been looking at the reasons God places us in Adversity University and the kind of coursework He prepares for us. Now, I want to give you a caution—the story of what happens when we decide to drop out of school. Yes, it is hard. Yes, it is difficult. Yes, it hurts. But, we have to stay in the race. The costs of dropping out are just too high.

We see that vividly illustrated in the life of Esau. What we are given is a two-sentence summary of the tragic consequences of dropping out of God's school, of forsaking the revealed will and plan of God for our lives, failing out of His University.

Change of Goals

First, when we drop out, our goals change. Verse fourteen tells us to "follow peace." This is a very strong word. In fact, in our New Testament it is most frequently translated as "persecute" because the idea of the word is to pursue with such determination that nothing can stop you from reaching the goal. Why was it important for Esau to follow peace? Esau was in a difficult family situation. His parents, Isaac and Rebekah, had to wait twenty years before they had children; and when they did, they had twins. Before they were born, God said that the elder would serve the younger. Esau was born first, which meant that according to God's plan, he would have to serve Jacob. If that were not enough, there was another area of contention. Isaac loved Esau, and Rebekah loved Jacob. It is dangerous for parents to show favoritism among their children, but that was the case in Esau's home.

Isaac and Esau loved the outdoors. You could have found them at Bass Pro Shop or Gander Mountain every weekend. They hunted and fished and worked together. Rebekah and Jacob were watching the Food Channel. Esau did not have a very good relationship with his mother or his brother, but he did have peace with his father. Now, pay careful attention to this—when Esau dropped out of school because of the adversity and hardship, he not only made his relationship with his mother and brother worse, but he also destroyed his relationship with his father. The peace was gone. Jacob was a deceiver, and he did wrong. He and Rebekah schemed to get Isaac to give the blessing to him instead of to Esau. But, Esau allowed that to knock him out of the race. (Remember that I told you most people quit because of other people.) Look at what Esau did.

When Esau saw that Isaac had blessed Jacob, and sent him away to Padan-aram, to take him a wife from thence; and that as he blessed him he gave him a charge, saying, Thou shalt not take a wife of the daughters of Canaan; And that Jacob obeyed his father and his mother, and was gone to Padan-aram; and Esau seeing that the daughters of Canaan pleased not Isaac his father; Then went Esau unto Ishmael, and took unto the wives which he had Mahalath the daughter of Ishmael Abraham's son, the sister of Nebajoth, to be his wife." (Genesis 28:6-9)

When he found out his father did not want his sons to marry a daughter of the Canaanites, Esau immediately went and married a heathen woman to spite his father. He did not care about maintaining peace in their relationship any more; his goals had changed. The very person he had wanted to please, he now wanted to bring pain. Peace with people can only come as a result of peace with God, and if you are a dropout, you will not be at peace with Him. What Esau did not realize was that by quitting, he forfeited both the goal of peace and the possibility of achieving it. I have had people tell me, "The reason we don't get along is because of him." No, the reason you do not get along is because of you and your improper relationship with God.

Peace is not the only goal. Verse fourteen not only tells us to follow peace; it also tells us to "follow holiness." Holiness is leading a sacred, pure, and blameless life. God has brought all the elements of your course work together with holiness as one of His primary goals. We saw that in Hebrews 12:10, we are chastened "for our profit that we might be partakers of his holiness." Holiness is a core attribute of the nature and character of God. If we drop out of school, we no longer have the potential to develop into holiness—becoming like Jesus Christ. We forfeit that goal.

Change of Insight

Second, when we drop out, our insights change. Verse fourteen also says "without which, no man shall see the Lord." When it talks about seeing God here, it is not talking about salvation. Hebrews is written to people who are already saved. It is talking about our vision of God; if you go back to verse two it says, "Looking unto Jesus." What we lose is the ability to see God in the midst of our adversity. As long as Peter looked at Jesus, he stayed on top of the water. When he focused on the storm and the waves, he started to sink. A place of adversity without Jesus is the loneliest place imaginable. We start looking around and ask, "Why is this happening to me? I don't understand." That is where we end up when we quit—blinded by the side of the track.

The second insight we lose is our discernment regarding what is happening to us. Verse 15 says, "Looking diligently lest any man fail of the grace of God." The grace of God never fails, so what is he talking about? He is saying that when we stop running the race, we stop appropriating God's grace for our lives. We can no longer see the offer He makes to step in and empower us for life. If you had asked Esau why he was angry, he probably would have said, "My mother is a crook. My brother is a deceiver. And my dad is so dumb, he fell for it. Jacob tricked me out of my birthright and stole my blessing. Why wouldn't I be mad?" He could not see that the root problem was his failure, not what others had done. Esau was not treated right, but God's grace would still have been sufficient for him to overcome that, if he had seen that he needed grace and asked God for it. Esau's failure was that he failed to seek, and receive, and live by the grace that God would have given to him if he would have simply asked for it. But, we forfeit our ability to see when we drop out.

The natural consequence of quitting is bitterness. You will not notice it at first (at lot of people never admit it!) because dropping out diminishes your insight. Notice the impact—"Lest any root of bitterness springing up trouble you." Bitterness does not just affect your life, it affects the life of everyone around you. And Esau was blind to the defilement he brought into his own family. His descendants became known as the Edomites, and they became bitter enemies against the people of God. They still are today, thirty-five hundred years later. The descendants of Esau are the inhabitants of modern day Jordan. If you fail to appropriate the grace of God by failing to stay in the race and enduring the education and training He has for us, the consequences will be sever and long-lasting. Our failure will contribute to the failures of others. What an awful thing to happen to a runner in God's race.

Change of Values

Third, when we drop out, our values change. The things that used to be important to us when we were right with God are suddenly not important anymore. Verse fifteen says, "Lest there be any fornicator..." That word "fornicator" is the Greek word pornos, from which we get the word pornography. The root meaning of the word is "to put up for sale." When we quit Adversity University, our values change so much that we are even willing to sell our purity and pollute our personal lives. Where once you wanted to be pure and holy from a heart of integrity, now you want to gratify your desires. If you love God properly, you would rather die than displease Him. Once you drop out, your values change. The things that once mattered before no longer matter to you.

Not only do we give up our purity when we drop out, but we also become profane people. We think of profanity as cursing, but the word actually comes from a word that means threshold. A. T. Robertson said it means "to take that which is holy and to put it under your feet and trample on it."

I have had people who used to come to our church and love their pastor give me obscene gestures when they saw me at the store! We have had people break into the church and steal things. How could they change so much? It is really simple; they dropped out, and it changed their values. Look at what Esau did; he sold his birthright, which should have been precious to him, for a single meal. He did not value that which was eternal; he valued that which was temporal.

Change of Future

Why did Esau do that? It was not because he was stupid. It was not because he did not know better. It was not because he wanted the rest of his life to be a long story of grief and disaster. It was not because he did not know what was right and what was wrong. It was all because he dropped out of school. And the changes in his goals, his insight, and his values changed his future. Esau could have become a great and godly man. His father and grandfather knew more about God than anyone else in the world. He could have learned to walk with God in faith, and there would have been seventeen names in Hebrews 11 instead of sixteen. We could read, "Esau accepted the difficult position of the elder serving the younger and became a great and godly man of faith."

But instead, verse seventeen says, "For ye know how that afterward, when he would have inherited the blessing, he was rejected: for he found no place of repentance, though he sought it carefully with tears." Esau cried and wept later, but today's decisions always affect tomorrow's experience. The consequences of our decisions are beyond our ability to calculate, and those consequences are beyond our ability to change... except through the mercy and grace of God. I am glad to tell you that you do not have to face the rest of your life as a drop out from God's University of Adversity. You can re-enroll.

Before you get back in school though, you are going to have to go back to the Master and beg for His forgiveness and candidly, transparently admit your sin. Let me tell you what that process is going to look like. He is going to test your sincerity and commitment by having you go back to the people who were impacted by your quitting and make things right with them. You may say that is impossible; and it is impossible in your own strength. But, if you do not fail of the grace of God, the grace of God will never fail you. He will help you make things right. Now, let's look at how we find God's grace.

21. Why Sinai Students Fail

"For ye are not come unto the mount that might be touched, and that burned with fire, nor unto blackness, and darkness, and tempest, And the sound of a trumpet, and the voice of words; which voice they that heard entreated that the word should not be spoken to them any more: (For they could not endure that which was commanded, And if so much as a beast touch the mountain, it shall be stoned, or thrust through with a dart: And so terrible was the sight, that Moses said, I exceedingly fear and quake:) But ye are come unto mount Sion, and unto the city of the living God, the heavenly Jerusalem, and to an innumerable company of angels." —Hebrews 12:18-22

Sinai or Sion?

There is a huge contrast between verse seventeen and verse eighteen. In the last chapter, we saw that Esau found no place of repentance. The word *place* is the Greek word *topos*, from which we get topography. Esau found no ground from which his circumstances could be changed. Now there are two options—two "grounds" that people can go to, and that is where verse eighteen picks up.

The author of Hebrews talks about "the mount" which, although he does not name it, is clearly Mount Sinai, where Moses received the Law from God. The children of Israel reached Mount Sinai exactly three months after they were miraculously delivered from Egyptian bondage. God brought them through the Red Sea and into the desert on the way to the land of promise. God covenanted with Abraham, and then confirmed to Isaac and Jacob that the land would belong to them. This land, which we know today as Israel, was a land that flowed with milk and honey. The second place, or ground, that people run to is Sion referenced in verse 22. Sion, or Zion, is another name for Jerusalem, the city that would become the capital of Israel, the city where Jesus would die for our sins. In this chapter, we are going to look at Sinai; and in next chapter, we will look at Sion.

Mount Sinai is in the Arabian Desert. God led the people there as a place of meeting. You can find the story of this momentous meeting in Exodus 19. God came down to the mountain of Sinai where the children of Israel were camped around the base. The people of God were afraid; because when God came down, there was lightning, thunder, and darkness. So, they asked if God would talk to Moses, and then Moses could tell them what God had to say. It was a frightening experience. If someone even touched the mountain, they would be killed. Even Moses was afraid. He said, "I exceedingly fear and quake." The people were at Mount Sinai so that God could give them the Law.

Law or Grace?

Why would the author of Hebrews talk about that experience in the context of Esau seeking and failing to find repentance? Because Sinai is not the answer! If you have failed and need to re-enroll in Adversity University, you will not find a place of repentance there. The message here is: do not go back to Sinai. Do not go back to that mountain; but rather, move forward into the Promised Land and come to Sion. You will never make progress in your Christian life if you remain at Mount Sinai.

In Galatians 4, Paul calls these two mountains an allegory regarding Law and Grace. So, when we study them, we have to understand that God is describing and contrasting two different approaches to trying to grow spiritually and succeed in the race. If you remain at Sinai in your spiritual life, then you are certain to become a miserable person and a failure.

Students at Sinai fail because they refuse to move forward. Mount Sinai was only intended to be a temporary experience for the children of Israel. God only wanted them to go to Sinai for a short period of time; they were never meant to live there. The problem with living at Sinai is that it gives us an incomplete view of God. We need to understand how they got to Sinai. The Israelites had been in Egypt for hundreds of years. God sent Moses to deliver them from bondage and slavery. After a series of plagues, God announced the final plague—the death of the firstborn. The oldest child in every house in Egypt would die, unless there was blood on the door posts. God said that when He came through the land, He would pass over those houses. It is from this promise that we get the name "Passover." How were the Israelites delivered? They were delivered through the blood. Each family took a lamb, killed it, and put the blood on the side posts and the top of the door. They had to do that through faith; nothing like this had ever happened before. But, those who responded to Moses' instructions were saved by the blood. This is such a beautiful picture of our salvation. Salvation is only through the shedding of the blood of the Lamb of God.

After the Passover, Pharaoh told the people to leave, and they did. Soon, they came to the Red Sea. Pharaoh regretted letting them go and came after them. God parted the waters, and people crossed the Red Sea on dry ground; then God closed the waters and destroyed the Egyptian army. First Corinthians 10:1-2 says, *"Moreover, brethren, I would not that ye should be ignorant, how that all our fathers were under the cloud, and all passed through the sea; And all were baptized unto Moses in the cloud and in the sea."* Here Paul tells us that crossing the Red Sea is a picture of baptism. They had water on both sides and water in the clouds above; so they were immersed, just as a person is when they are baptized. The example we see here is the process of spiritual growth. First, we see the Israelites at the Passover (picturing salvation), then the Red Sea, (picturing baptism), and finally they came to Mount Sinai.

At this point in their spiritual walk, they did not know much about God. They saw Him as distant and unapproachable. What God was doing at Mount Sinai, in addition to giving them the Law, was establishing in their minds the fundamental attribute of His character. God fundamentally, first and foremost, is Holy. When God showed Isaiah and John a glimpse of Heaven, they both saw four angels flying around the throne of God crying out "Holy, Holy, Holy." This is what God has chosen to emphasize because it is so central to His nature. By the way, the holiness of God is what makes the miracle of salvation so amazing. He gave us His Son as the perfect Lamb to take away the sin of the world, so that we could come into His presence.

That is the vital lesson that Sinai misses. At Mount Sinai, God is still unapproachable. Yes, we must learn and apply the truth that God is holy, but we cannot stop there. If that is all you know, you have a warped idea of God and Christianity. You can tell people who are stuck at Sinai, because they are always trying to reduce Christianity to a set of rules. "You can't do this and you have to do that." It is all about the rules. That is not God's way for you to live. You need to get beyond Sinai and go on to Sion. But remember, you cannot get to Sion without going to Sinai first. God's holiness is a vital and foundational truth; it is just not the whole truth.

Rules or Relationship?

What major task was given to the children of Israel at Sinai? It was not the law! In fact, if you read Exodus 19 to 31, you will find that most of the instructions given to Moses had nothing to do with the law. Most of the time that God spent with Moses was focused on preparing to build a house of worship. God leads us step by step. We get saved (Passover), we get baptized (Red Sea), we learn how holy God is (Mount Sinai), and then we are supposed to move on. When I went to college, one of the first things they did was give me a student handbook. In it were all the rules and instructions for how students were supposed to live at the school. God promised the people that if they would live according to the handbook, He would bless them. *"Now therefore, if ye will obey my voice indeed, and keep my covenant, then ye shall be a peculiar treasure unto me above all people: for all the earth is mine: And ye shall be unto me a kingdom of priests, and an holy nation. These are the words which thou shalt speak unto the children of Israel."* (Exodus 19:5-6)

But, while the rules are vital, they are not enough. We are not ready to move on from Sinai until we are ready to worship. No one ever gets beyond the concept of God as distant and unapproachable until they develop a personal worship relationship with God. The trap so many people fall into is that they substitute the rules for the relationship. But, without worship, it is not long before the rules start to feel restrictive. This version of the Christian life is miserable. "God doesn't want me to have any fun." No, that is the wrong view. God wants you to rejoice in Him. God never intended for you to live it at Sinai. He said to Moses, "Let Me tell you the rules and how things are to be done. But then let Me also show you how you can worship Me. Let's go to the tabernacle and I'll lead you to the Promised Land."

Sinai students are failures because they are living in the wrong place.

They are stuck without the worship relationship with God that gives life joy, purpose, meaning, and fulfillment. No wonder they are so miserable! So many people today are confused about what Sinai means, and their confusion causes them to fail. For example, many people think they can gain merit and favor with God by the things they do or do not do. That is not what the law was for. It was never given for salvation; it was for the orderliness of their society and to enhance their walk with God. You are saved by the shed blood of Jesus Christ, God's Son, or you are not saved at all. No one is saved by works. It is either one or the other.

The failure of Sinai students is vividly illustrated for us in Exodus 32. Moses stayed on the mountain with God for forty days, and the people began to think that he was not going to come back. They went to Aaron and demanded that he make them an idol that they could worship. New believers are very vulnerable to cults and false teaching. It is easy for them to be swayed from the truth. That is because they do not yet have a deep relationship with God. The Israelites thought that because God was silent, He was not present. That is not true. He is always there with you. God's delays do not indicate God's disinterest. But if you live at Sinai, where you are just trying to keep rules instead of worshipping God, that is what you are going to think. The end result of staying at Sinai is idolatry. You may not make a golden calf or join a cult, but there are many people who worship their rules. That always leads to failure. Your personal and corporate worship of God are the next step along the path God has laid out for you. Build a tabernacle and start to worship. Do not stop at Sinai!

22. Why Sion Students Succeed

"For ye are not come unto the mount that might be touched, and that burned with fire, nor unto blackness, and darkness, and tempest, And the sound of a trumpet, and the voice of words; which voice they that heard entreated that the word should not be spoken to them any more: (For they could not endure that which was commanded, And if so much as a beast touch the mountain, it shall be stoned, or thrust through with a dart: And so terrible was the sight, that Moses said, I exceedingly fear and quake:) But ye are come unto mount Sion, and unto the city of the living God, the heavenly Jerusalem, and to an innumerable company of angels." —Hebrews 12:18-22

From Sinai Campus to Sion Campus

We looked at Sinai—the importance of grasping the holiness and requirements of God, and the vital role that worship plays in our lives. Now let's look at how we can succeed by reaching Sion. There are three keys to the success of Sion students, those who have left the Sinai campus of Adversity University and reached the Sion campus.

Sion students succeed because they move on from Sinai. What helps us transition from law to grace, from works to worship, from struggle to success, and from burden to blessing? It is simply moving ahead. Sion is another name for the city of Jerusalem. You cannot get to Sion without first going to Sinai. You must understand and establish God's holiness before you move on. Sinai educated us in God's laws. It is there that we learn the vital importance of both personal and corporate worship. Once that is done, what is next? Your focus needs to be on developing a dynamic personal relationship with the Lord Jesus Christ.

It is important to realize that, despite what some people teach and the words we find in some hymns, getting into Canaan is not a picture of going to Heaven. Canaan represents victorious Christian living—there are still battles to be fought, but God gives the victory. I do not want to stand on Jordan's stormy banks and cast a wishful eye; I want to get in! A whole generation of Israelites saw the Promised Land but died in the wilderness. I do not want to just wander in the wilderness. That is a picture of a Christian who never develops, grows, and matures. God took care of the children of Israel. He fed them, and He clothed them because they were His children; but they missed out on Sion. They missed out on the Promised Land. What a tragedy! So many Christians have a sour, dour attitude about God, about Christianity, and about church because they are stuck in the wilderness, having never moved on from Sinai.

Sion Campus – A Place of Faith

Sion students succeed because they exercise their faith. Out of all the perhaps two to three million Israelites, only two adult men got in to the country where Sion is, Joshua and Caleb. Moses sent twelve men in to spy out the land. Ten of them came back saying that, while the land was blessed with abundant crops, the inhabitants were too strong to defeat. Only Joshua and Caleb trusted in God and believed that He would give them the victory. As a result of their lack of faith, the entire generation perished in the wilderness without ever reaching Sion. When the forty years of wandering were over, God brought them back to the border and placed another test in front of them. By the way, before you get to Sion, you can count on it that God will put an impossibility in your path just as He did to them.

The first test the Israelites faced was the Jordan River. When they reached the Jordan, it was in flood stage—half a mile wide with swift currents so that, humanly speaking, there was no way across. God told Joshua to have the priests carry the Ark of the Covenant out into the water. It was not until they actually got their feet wet that God parted the water. That is faith being exercised! And the tests did not end once they crossed the river. They had to face the walled city of Jericho, then a coalition of five kings and giants...and the list goes on and on. As we have already seen, God increases our faith by exercising it and adding challenges to make us stronger. We cannot reach Sion without putting our faith into action.

You cannot get to know God and become a dynamic believer without having your faith stretched. The level of faith you have today will not be sufficient next year. God is going to make sure that problems, people, or pressures are going to continue to intensify in your life. The exercise of your faith is well worth it, because in each and every event where God brings adversity and we respond by faith, we get to see the greatness of our God. Moses said, *"O Lord God, thou hast begun to shew thy servant thy greatness, and thy mighty hand: for what God is there in heaven or in earth, that can do according to thy works, and according to thy might?"* (Deuteronomy 3:24) Because of Moses' faith, he had a front row seat—the burning bush, the plagues in Egypt, the parting of the Red Sea, manna in the wilderness, water from the rock—the list goes on and on. Even with all of the miracles of God's mighty hand, Moses said it was only the beginning of God's greatness. If we refuse to move forward in faith, then we forfeit the opportunity to have our faith stretched and see God in all His miraculous power.

Sion Campus – A Place of Sacrifice

Sion students succeed because they sacrifice. Sion has great historical significance. It was a place where God's people came to offer sacrifices unto Him. Sion is where Abraham took his son Isaac, and they built an altar. There, Isaac lay on that altar; and Abraham willing to sacrifice his son, but God sent a ram which was a picture of Jesus Christ. Sion is where David bought the threshing floor of Araunah to offer a sacrifice to God after he sinned by numbering the people. He said, *"Neither will I offer burnt offerings unto the Lord my God of that which doth cost me nothing."* (2 Samuel 24:24) Most importantly, Sion is the place where the Lamb of God, Jesus Christ, was crucified. One of the reasons you continue to grow spiritually after arriving in Sion is that it is a place of making sacrifice unto God. If you want to be a student of God in the campus of Sion, then you must be prepared to make sacrifices. There is no way you will ever endure the adversity unless you are a sacrificial giver. Sacrifice involves so much more than just money. We ought to tithe; we ought to give offerings unto the Lord, but we ought to live our lives sacrificially for God. It is only when we are willing to sacrifice that we maximize our potential for spiritual development and growth.

Sion Campus – A Place Called Home

Sion students succeed because they make Sion their home. Verse twenty-two says, *"But ye are come unto mount Sion."* That phrase in the language of the Bible is very precise. It is not talking about coming for visit; it is talking about moving in to a permanent residence. The idea is to decide that you are going to live in the presence of God. If you read John 15, you will see Jesus talking about abiding in Him. That is what this verse means. Coming to Sion means that we are living in the presence of Jesus. After a long day at work, I look forward to going home. That is a place a of refuge for me. Dianne and I love each other, and so we want to spend time together.

We often forget that while those of us who are saved have an eternal future waiting for us in Heaven, we also have the obligation and opportunity to live in Sion—"the heavenly Jerusalem" right now. Do not live in isolation from God. Do not view Him as being distant and unapproachable as the people did at Sinai. Jesus has opened the way into His presence through His blood. That means you and I can have the same kind of dynamic relationship with God here on earth that we will enjoy in Heaven. By the grace of God, we can live in Sion and be successful students in Adversity University.

23. WHERE DO YOU LIVE?

"But ye are come unto mount Sion, and unto the city of the living God, the heavenly Jerusalem, and to an innumerable company of angels, To the general assembly and church of the firstborn, which are written in heaven, and to God the Judge of all, and to the spirits of just men made perfect, And to Jesus the mediator of the new covenant, and to the blood of sprinkling, that speaketh better things than that of Abel." —Hebrews 12:22-24

When I read these verses, I think of a real estate agent describing a prime piece of property, listing all of the advantages that will come with making a move. We have talked about the two different choices for places to live—Sinai and Sion.

There are so many advantages for the child of God who lives right now in the same kind of relationship with God that we will have in the eternal home where we will live forever. Then it will be wonderful, but we need help today! So, we need to live in Sion. Like everything else in the Christian life, we do that by faith. Abraham left his home, looking for the city whose Builder and Maker is God. We need to turn our gaze and our focus toward that celestial city by meditating on where we live, spiritually speaking.

As God describes His children and their dwelling and their lives in this passage, He blends together the present and the future, and He forgets the past. I am so glad He does! God, who lives in eternity, looks at you and I as already being seated in the heavens beside Him. Our part is to live by faith, accepting and claiming what God has declared to already be true. No, we cannot see it yet with our eyes, but faith sees what is invisible. Let's look at the privileges of those who live in Zion.

Sion – Lack of Prejudice

First, **there is no prejudice to those who live in Zion**. It is true that the book of Hebrews was written predominantly for Hebrew people, but the promises are for everyone who is a believer. God is not prejudiced. Sion is not simply for the Jew. Now, in Christ we are one. The Scripture says we are no longer Jew, Gentile, Greek, bond, free, male, or female; we are all one in Christ. (Galatians 3:28) That means all of us can enjoy all of the privileges of this relationship with God through faith in Christ. The world may be divided by racial and ethnic prejudice, but Jesus erased all of those divisions.

Wherefore remember, that ye being in time past Gentiles in the flesh, who are called Uncircumcision by that which is called the Circumcision in the flesh made by hands; That at that time ye were without Christ, being aliens from the commonwealth of Israel, and strangers from the covenants of promise, having no hope, and without god in the world: But now in Christ Jesus ye who sometimes were far off are made nigh by the blood of Christ. For he is our peace, who hath made both one, and hath broken down the middle wall of partition between us; Having abolished in his flesh the enmity, even the law of commandments contained in ordinances; for to make in himself of twain one new man, so making peace. (Ephesians 2:11-15)

This is a wonderful promise from God. There is no prejudice in Sion. All of us, regardless of our background, race, or ethnic identity, are one in Christ. No matter what we have done in the past, it has been washed by the blood of Christ. It will never be remembered or held against us again. There are no second-class citizens in Heaven. You can dwell there close to God. I remember Brother Lester Roloff singing:

> *Thank God there was a fountain opened*
> And the blood of God's dear Son
> *Purifies the soul and reaches*
> *Deeper than the stain has gone.*
> *Praise the Lord for full salvation*
> *God still lives upon His throne,*
> *And I know the blood still reaches*
> *Deeper than the stain has gone.*

Even if you have wandered far away from God, you have a place to come home to called Sion. It does not matter what your background is. It does not matter who your parents were. None of those things matter in God's family. He is your Father, and Jesus is your older brother. There are a lot of people who, even though they have been set free, are still living under the old bondage. During the Civil War, Abraham Lincoln signed the Emancipation Proclamation, declaring all of the slaves in the South to be free. However, most of them did not know it; and though they were legally free, they still lived as slaves. As the Union Army advanced through the South, they carried with them copies of the document to let the slaves know they had been released from bondage. God has set you free—live like it! Rejoice in the privileges God has given to you as His child.

Sion - Premier Location

Second, **Sion offers us an incredible location**. In the real-estate business, they say that the three most important factors in pricing a property are location, location, and location. Well, look at Sion's location. Verse twenty-two says we are come *"unto the city of the living God."* You cannot beat that! The Greek word used here for *city* means "a community with walls." In Bible times, walls were vital to the defense of a city. Without them, you had no means of security or protection. Compare that to Sinai. In the wasteland of the desert, there were no defenses. It was wide open—every man for himself. There was no law, no order, no security, and no safety. Now, we have a home in the city of the living God.

When I was growing up, my parents liked to take us camping. I really enjoyed it. So, when Dianne and I first started talking about getting married, since we did not have a whole lot of money, I thought I would take her camping for our honeymoon. (That may not be the dumbest idea I've had in my life, but it's got to be pretty close!) Do you know what I found out? I found out she did not like camping, not even a little bit. In fact, she told me, "Camping to me, Paul, is staying in a Motel 6 instead of a Holiday Inn!" Why would you camp at Sinai when you have reservations in Sion, the city of the living God, waiting for you? Why "rough it" when you can enjoy luxury? Why not trade self-reliance for God's safety and security? Move into Sion—the city of the living God!

Sinai is where God came to visit, remember? In Exodus 19, God came down from His city where He lives and visited Sinai. It was a wonderful thing, kind of scary, but it was where He gave the law. He said, "Listen, come not just to a place where God visits, but come to a place where God lives." That is a wonderful, wonderful promise from God's Word.

Sion – Enduring Construction

Third, **Sion offers us an enduring home.** Buildings built here on earth are subject to decay. Over time, the elements and the wear and tear of use make our buildings grow old and decay. But, Sion is built with materials that will last. The Bible says that each gate of the Holy City is made from a single pearl. A thousand-year-old pearl is just as strong and beautiful as a brand new one. It does not age or decay. The street of Heaven is made with pure gold. If you have some 500-year-old gold that you want to get rid of because it is old, bring it by my house! Gold does not age or decay. All the materials used in the new Jerusalem are perfect, because everything in Heaven is a perfect. By the way, if we keep that in mind—that we are heading for an enduring home—we will not get so bent out of shape about what's happening in the here and now.

The Bible starts with Eden, a beautiful and perfect place where Adam and Eve lived. From the beginning God's creation was "very good." Sin entered the picture and wrecked our world. We struggle with those consequences still today. But the Bible also ends with a beautiful and perfect place. The home God is preparing for us in His presence has been under construction for a long time. Jesus said, *"I go to prepare a place for you. And if I go and prepare a place for you, I will come again, and receive you unto myself; that where I am there ye may be also."* (John 14:2-3) The prepared place is our enduring home.

Sion – Wonderful Neighbors

Fourth, **Sion provides us wonderful neighbors.** Verse twenty-two says that in Heaven there is "an innumerable company of angels." Heaven is filled with angels praising and worshiping God. Oh, what wonderful neighbors! Verse twenty-three says, we will also live with *"the general assembly and church of the firstborn."* In Bible days, the firstborn son received the greatest blessings and the largest share of the inheritance. What God is telling us here is that through His grace, we get to share in all the privileges of His firstborn Son. All the believers of all the ages will be our neighbors. Sometimes, Christians do not get along very well here on earth. But, there all of us will be perfect; we will get along wonderfully with all of our neighbors.

Sion – Presence of God

Best of all, in the new Sion, we will be in the presence of God. Verse twenty-three says, *"to God the Judge of all."* There will be so many wonderful things in Heaven. I cannot wait to see the gates of pearl and the street of gold. And, I want to know if the crystal river is stocked with trout! But, all of the beauty and wonder will pale in comparison to being in the presence of Almighty God. Right now in our sinful state, seeing God would literally kill us. When Moses asked to see Him, God replied, *"Thou canst not see my face: for there shall no man see me, and live."* (Exodus 33:20) In fact, just seeing God from the back after He had passed by made Moses' face glow so brightly that he had to wear a veil to talk to the Israelites.

And our beautiful Savior will be there in Sion. Verse twenty-four says, *"And to Jesus the mediator of the new covenant."* Now, there are many different names and titles of Jesus, but here He is called the Mediator of the new covenant. The old covenant was the Mosaic Covenant—given at Sinai. God gave Moses the law, but the law never saved a soul and never brought peace to a broken heart. Jesus came to bring a new covenant. He not only provided for the covering of sins which the sacrifices had done; He provided for the cleansing of sins, which animal sacrifices could never do. A mediator is someone who brings harmony between two parties that are at war. We were at war with God over our sins. We are sinners by nature, and we are sinners by choice. But Jesus stepped in and mediated between God and man. In Sion, we get to live in His presence. Why would anyone live in Sinai? Come live in Sion with its lack of prejudice, its wonderful location, its enduring construction, and its wonderful neighbors.

24. TALKING BLOOD

"But ye are come unto mount Sion, and unto the city of the living God, the heavenly Jerusalem, and to an innumerable company of angels, To the general assembly and church of the firstborn, which are written in heaven, and to God the Judge of all, and to the spirits of just men made perfect, And to Jesus the mediator of the new covenant, and to the blood of sprinkling, that speaketh better things than that of Abel." —Hebrews 12:22-24

Christ's Blood vs. Abel's Blood

We know that we are weak, frail, failing students in God's school, Adversity University. Yet, we also know that God expects us to endure chastening, keep running the race, and receive a good report through faith as we grow and mature in Him. How is that possible? How can sinful people live victorious lives? How can we be overcomers? The answer is found in verse twenty-four. Our successful running of the race, our maturing, our faith, indeed our very salvation is found in the precious blood of Jesus Christ.

The phrase "the blood of sprinkling" goes back to Old Testament days. Once a year, on the Day of Atonement, the high priest would take the blood into the Holy of Holies and sprinkle it on the mercy seat. Jesus Christ was both our High Priest and our sacrifice. (Hebrews 9:12)

It is through the shedding of Christ's blood that we have the forgiveness of our sins, and that blood gives us salvation – eternal, everlasting life. But, salvation is not the last time we need the sprinkling of the blood. That is not the last time we sin. I got saved when I was five years of age, so most my sins of my life were committed after I was saved. I do not need to get saved again and again and again. The blood of Jesus Christ cleanses us from all sin at salvation. But, we need a new sprinkling of the blood for our sins after salvation. First John 1:7 declares, *"But if we walk in the light, as he is in the light, we have fellowship one with another, and the blood of Jesus Christ his Son cleanseth us from all sin."* The blood speaks. Verse twenty-four says that Christ's blood speaks better things than Abel's blood. So let's compare the two, and see what they have to say. In Genesis 4, we see the first murder in human history. Abel was killed by his own brother, Cain.

Cry of Abel's Blood – Justice

And Cain talked with Abel his brother: and it came to pass, when they were in the field, that Cain rose up against Abel his brother, and slew him. And the Lord said unto Cain, Where is Abel thy brother? And he said, I know not: Am I my brother's keeper? And he said, What hast thou done? The voice of thy brother's blood crieth unto me from the ground. And now art thou cursed from the earth, which hath opened her mouth to receive thy brother's blood from thy hand;" (Genesis 4:8-11)

I believe that when Cain slew Abel, he probably buried Abel's body and thought, "I've gotten away with this." But, he did not get away with anything. God confronted Cain for his evil deed. God said, "I heard a voice. I heard the voice of some precious, righteous blood." In Matthew 23:25, Jesus Himself talks about the blood of righteous Abel. Abel was a man who loved God and lived for God and served

God. When he was slain, his righteous blood cried out to God. Based on God's response to Cain in verse eleven, Abel's blood cried out to God and said, "Justice! Vengeance!" So God, responding to the voice of Abel's blood, came down, and confronted Cain. He said, "Cain, you've sinned. Because you murdered your brother, I am going to punish you with a curse." Cain said, "This is more than I can bear." Abel's blood cried out for justice—with good reason. But, I am so glad that there is another blood crying out with its voice.

Cry of Christ's Blood – Mercy

Like Cain, we are all responsible for murder—the death of the Lord Jesus Christ on the cross. Jesus' blood has every right to cry out to the Father for eternal vengeance against each one of us. Without the sprinkling of the blood of Christ on the mercy seat, we would still be condemned under the old covenant. That is why verse twenty-four says that Christ's blood speaks better things than Abel's blood. The blood of Jesus cries out for mercy and forgiveness. We deserve God's wrath, but the blood speaks for our pardon. We talked earlier about the high priest sprinkling the blood on the mercy seat, but the tradition of salvation by sprinkled blood goes back even further than that.

On the night of the first Passover, each Jewish family was instructed to take the blood of a lamb, put it in a basin, dip a hyssop branch in the blood, and sprinkle the blood on the top and sides of the door. This act of faith and obedience spared their firstborn children from death. The blood spoke for their covering. Thousands of years later, Jesus Christ was crucified on the very night of the Hebrew celebration of the Passover. He was, as John the Baptist announced, the Passover Lamb that took away the sins of the world. The blood of the Passover lambs, and the blood the high priest sprinkled on the mercy seat only covered sin; Jesus' blood cleanses sin! Sins that are only covered can be brought back against us again. Sins that are cleansed are gone forever. God says concerning those sins, *"I will remember them no more."* (Hebrews 8:12)

Ark of the Covenant

To understand fully what Jesus' blood says, we have to understand the Ark of the Covenant. As part of the instructions for worship that God gave to Moses in the book of Exodus, he was told to make a special box that would go in the tabernacle. Exodus 25:8-9 says, *"And let them make me a sanctuary; that I may dwell among them. According to all that I shew thee, after the pattern of the tabernacle."* You cannot build the tabernacle on earth after the pattern of the tabernacle unless there is another tabernacle to be patterned after. The instructions God gave to Moses allowed him to recreate on earth a picture of what is in Heaven. If you read on through Exodus 25, you will see very specific instructions for the size, shape, and composition of the Ark of the Covenant, and the rest of the items that would go into the tabernacle. The pattern that God gave Moses for worship followed the pattern from Heaven. If you read Hebrews 9 and 10, you will see how the sacrifices in the tabernacle picture what Jesus Christ would later do.

The High Priest

The steps that the high priest followed were followed by Jesus Christ. He died as the Lamb, shedding His blood on the cross; then, as our High Priest, He took His perfect, pure, and sinless blood to the mercy seat in the real tabernacle in Heaven and sprinkled it there for us. That is the blood that still speaks better things today. His blood does not call out an eye for an eye or a tooth for a tooth. Jesus' blood cries out to the Father, "Give them mercy! Give them mercy! Give them mercy!"

We will fail as students of Adversity University unless we learn to go frequently to the throne room, fall down before the mercy seat, and cry out for forgiveness. First John 1:9 tells us that God is faithful to forgive us when we confess our sins. We do not need to be saved again, but we do need His ongoing mercy and forgiveness, and we receive it because of the blood.

Every single student fails some of the tests in Adversity University. What do we do? Do we throw our hands in the air and give up? Do we say, "I quit. There's no hope for me. I've blown it."? No. Repent of your sin and run to the mercy seat. There, Jesus destroyed the power of the devil. *"Forasmuch then as the children are partakers of flesh and blood, he also himself likewise took part of the same; that through death he might destroy him that had the power of death, that is, the devil."* (Hebrews 2:14) The devil still exists, but he has already been destroyed. His power over us has been broken. I no longer have to fear because Jesus' blood conquered the devil. At the mercy seat, Jesus also delivered us from fear. *"And deliver them who through fear of death were all their lifetime subject to bondage."* (Hebrews 2:15) The devil wants us to doubt. He wants us to be afraid. However, the blood gives us confidence. God does not trade you in or give up on you when you sin. He says, "You're Mine, and you're Mine for keeps. It's not because you're doing well. I keep you the same way I saved you. I didn't save you because of your good works; I saved you because I saw My Son's blood. I listened to His blood rather than Abel's blood, and I extended mercy instead of justice."

The blood of God's Son is what allows us to live with a clear conscience. *"How much more shall the blood of Christ, who through the eternal Spirit offered himself without spot to God, purge your conscience from dead works to serve the living God?"* (Hebrews 9:14) So many people are weighed down by guilt for the things they have done or failed to do. The devil uses that against them to keep them burdened down. The blood of Christ can purge your conscience and free you from the weight of guilt. You do not have to carry it any more. Yes, there are things we may regret or be ashamed of, but the guilt is gone. The Apostle Paul was responsible for the death of many, many believers; and yet, he became a dynamic, vibrant spokesman for Christ. He was able to hold his head up high and preach the glorious gospel message of Jesus Christ because he found forgiveness through the shedding of Christ's blood.

Assurance in His Blood

But the blood provides more than just our salvation. Hebrews 10:10 says, *"By the which will we are sanctified through the offering of the body of Jesus Christ once for all."* My sanctification, my perfection, my maturing is absolutely, completely guaranteed because of that sprinkled blood. There are two ways for our sanctification to be completed. We can cooperate with God, repent of sins, and stay close to the mercy seat; or He can take us to Heaven early. In either case, everyone who is saved will one day stand before God perfected. The blood assures it. We will have glorified bodies, and everything from earth will be in the past. I believe that God is going to erase, not just the tears from our eyes, but also the evil from our memories. We are going to be able to serve Him perfectly forever and ever and ever. Why? Not because we are anything special, but because one day the Son of God sprinkled His blood on the mercy seat, and it speaks for us.

How do we appropriate the power of that blood? Hebrews 10:19-20 says, *"Having therefore, brethren, boldness to enter into the holiest by the blood of Jesus, By a new and living way."* We can have boldness to enter in, even when we have sinned. We can come before the throne, but what do we do when we get there?

Seeing then that we have a great high priest, that is passed into the heavens, Jesus the Son of God, let us hold fast our profession. For we have not an high priest which cannot be touched with the feeling of our infirmities; but was in all points tempted like as we are, yet without sin. Let us therefore come boldly unto the throne of grace, that we may obtain mercy, and find grace to help in time of need. (Hebrews 4:14-16)

Run to the Mercy Seat

When was the last time you went to the throne of grace and asked for mercy? We all sin. The problem is too many people sin and then say, "Well, that's too bad." How many times I have heard, "I just couldn't help myself." Our natural tendency is to make excuses instead of repenting and asking for mercy. But, if we make excuses for our sin, we are certain to begin to fail in Adversity University. Our A's will go to B's, our B's will go to C's, and our C's will go to D's. It will not be long before our hearts are cold and hardened and we are far away from God. Instead, we need to be running to the throne of mercy. We need to come there, and we need to confess our sins. We need to forsake them and say, "Dear God, I'm not coming to you because of anything worthy in and of myself, but I'm asking for Your mercy."

When we do that, the Son of God says, "Father, I know what this man is going through. I was tempted in all points just like he is. I know what this sister is going through, the discouragement she's feeling right now, and the regret. I know the temptation to which she has yielded. I never yielded to temptation, but he is yielded to it, she is yielded to it. Oh Father, on the basis of My blood that I sprinkled on the mercy seat, I ask you to forgive them. I ask you to give them mercy. They do not deserve it, Father, but give it to them. Do not listen to Abel's blood; listen to My blood and give them mercy." The Bible promises that we will obtain mercy; and, in addition, we will find grace to help in our time of need.

The path on which you travel to get mercy ought to be well worn, but the tragedy of many Christians is that they are so busy, so caught up in their lives, and so unconscious of wickedness that they forsake that path. But, apart from that path, we miss out on the mercy, we miss out on the grace, and we slide away from God. The only way back to an intimate relationship with Him is to get back on that path. Those Christians who are closest to God are close to Him because they are often at His throne seeking mercy. When we are distant from God, it is because we have sin in our lives, and we are not coming to Him and dealing with it, confessing it, and finding His mercy. The blood of Christ speaks better things than the blood of Abel. I will take Christ's blood, how about you? I do not want justice, I need mercy. Thank God we can find it at the throne of grace.

25. Listen To Your Teacher

"See that ye refuse not him that speaketh. For if they escaped not who refused him that spake on earth, much more shall not we escape, if we turn away from him that speaketh from heaven:" —Hebrews 12:25

I heard about a little boy who was not getting good grades in school because he had not been paying attention to his teacher. One day, his teacher sent a note home for his parents about his conduct and his grades. The next day, he came up to the teacher and said, "I don't want to scare you, but my dad told me last night that if I don't start getting better grades somebody's going to get a spanking!" That kid needs a dunce cap. The teacher is not the problem. Bad things happen when we do not pay attention. I do not know how many times someone has sat in my office who was desperately seeking help, and I heard them say, "I wish I had listened." This concept of listening is not just hearing; the idea is listening with the full intention of heeding what is said.

He Speaks through His Blood

First, **God speaks to us through Jesus' blood**. The alternative to listening is refusing to hear. That is what the children of Israel did at Mount Sinai. They asked for God to speak to Moses because they did not want to hear His voice. The warning here is very stern. If we refuse to heed God when He speaks to our hearts, as he calls us and challenges us to this matter of growth and maturity and perfection, then we are treading on very dangerous ground.

You and I must not refuse the One who shed His blood on Calvary's cross for our sins. Today, when Jesus speaks to you, He speaks with nail prints in His hands and feet. He speaks with the marks from the crown of thorns in His brow. He speaks with the wound in His side. I can imagine Him saying, "Why would you refuse Me? After all I have done for you, why would you turn your back on Me? Why would you quit My will? Why would you quit My work? Why would you quit My way? Why would you go into the world after all I have done for you? My blood was shed for you! Can you not then live for Me?"

When we refuse to listen to the voice of our Saviour, we are refusing the Saviour who shed His precious blood for our sins. I have known some people who said they were Christians, but they appeared to be content with simply having a fire insurance policy against going to Hell. They do not read the Bible or go out soul winning or spend time serving God. They are having a good time in the world and living it up, but I want to tell you that there is a judgment day coming. Such people may be backslidden believers, or they may not be saved at all. Jesus issued a solemn warning to us in the Sermon on the Mount regarding people who think they are saved but do not truly have a personal relationship with Him.

Not every one that saith unto me, Lord, Lord, shall enter into the kingdom of heaven; but he that doeth the will of my Father which is in heaven. Many will say to me in that day, Lord, Lord, have we not prophesied in thy name? and in thy name have cast out devils? and in thy name done many wonderful works? And then will I profess unto them, I never knew you: depart from me, ye that work iniquity. (Matthew 7:21-23)

There are so many blessings that come along with our salvation as we serve the Lord. We experience spiritual growth and development, a personal walk with God, answers to prayer, the opportunity to see our lives used, and the joy of being a blessing to others. All of those blessings are forfeited when we walk away from Adversity University, because we refuse to listen to the Teacher who speaks to us through His blood.

He Speaks through His Word

Second, **God speaks to us through His Word.** Hebrews 12:5 says, *"And ye have forgotten the exhortation which speaketh unto you as unto children..."* The rest of verse five and all of verse six are a quotation from Proverbs 3:11-12. That is a reminder that God speaks to us through His Word. When we open the Bible with its 1,189 chapters and 773,466 inspired words, we are not simply reading the writings of Paul, the writings of Peter, or the writings of John—it is the eternal Word of the Living God. The Bible is not simply a statistical book of historical significance; it is contemporary to every generation, every individual, and every situation and circumstance in life.

Notice that the Bible does not use a past tense verb when referring to the Word. It is *speaking*. It is present, active, and living in our lives today. The Holy Spirit of God takes a word or a passage from Scripture and speaks to our hearts. Our responsibility is not to take that Word lightly. When the Bible is read or preached, and when we memorize and meditate on it, we are listening to God's voice. The decision we must make is what we are going to do with what God speaks to us through His Word. The most dangerous thing we can do is to reject what He says to us. I have heard people say, "I didn't make a decision." You did make a decision if you said, "No." The root word translated *refuse* in this verse means to "turn and run away." Every time we reject God's voice, our hearts get harder, and it gets easier to say, "No." We need to immediately respond in obedience by faith every time we hear His voice.

He Speaks through His Spirit

Third, **God speaks to us through His Spirit.** Hebrews 3:7-8 says, *"Wherefore as the Holy Ghost saith, To day if ye will hear his voice, Harden not your hearts."* Often, we get so busy in our lives, that we do not take time to listen to God. We do not allow Him to speak to our hearts. In all of the action and activity of life, we must carve out, on a regular basis, quiet time where we can listen to God. Before we launch out to face the adversity and pressure of the day, we need to allow Him to speak to us. Every child of God has the internal voice of the Spirit of God speaking. That voice is the voice of the Author of the Scripture. He will take the Word and apply it to our lives, if we will heed His voice.

The Holy Spirit makes application of what we read and hear, and helps us interpret the Scriptures correctly. It is miraculous that God takes the same Bible and applies it to the individual lives of millions of believers all around the world.

All of us, regardless of how long we have been saved and what our spiritual maturity level is, have different struggles and issues and problems that we are facing. God also knows what problems we will face in the future.

Many times, people have said to me, "Pastor Kingsbury, something I heard from God last Sunday really helped me this week." That was the Spirit applying the Word to someone's heart in advance to prepare them for adversity. If you are so busy, with so much activity going on, that you cannot take time to prepare your heart for the Spirit to teach you what you need to learn, you are going to miss out on His training and the benefit of His encouragement and teaching to help you live the Christian life.

He Speaks through Others

Fourth, **God speaks to us through the testimony of faithful believers.** Hebrews 3:13 says, *"But exhort one another daily while it is called To day; lest any of you be hardened through the deceitfulness of sin."* God's plan is for us to encourage and uplift each other. He speaks to us through other believers. Thank God for those people who care enough about you to come alongside and say, "Listen, you need to change this. You need to dedicate your life to Christ. You need to serve Him with your whole heart." Sometimes, people resent those who correct them; that is foolish and dangerous. God is speaking to you through their words.

Also, understand that if you are listening to the voice of the Spirit of God and walking in fellowship with the Lord, God wants to use you to encourage others. Your words and your testimony and your encouragement can make the difference for another believer who is struggling with adversity. Proverbs 25:11 says, *"A word fitly spoken is like apples of gold in pictures of silver."* So often we speak rashly, without thinking about the impact of our words. If we speak through the flesh instead of the Spirit, we have a negative impact on the other runners in the race. God wants us to encourage and exhort each other.

It is interesting that this is not meant to be an occasional action—God says to do it *"daily."* You can be walking in fellowship with God on Saturday and be walking away from God on Sunday. We need daily exhortation. Not only can we be inspired by living believers; but we can also learn from the pattern and example of those who have gone before. Hebrews 11:4 says, *"By faith Abel offered unto God a more excellent sacrifice than Cain, by which he obtained witness that he was righteous, God testifying of his gifts: and by it he being dead yet speaketh."* Abel has been in Heaven for thousands of years, yet his testimony of faith still encourages us today. Your testimony, whether good or bad, will outlive your life.

I first heard Richard Wurmbrand speak when I was sixteen years old. He was a pastor in Romania, who spent fourteen years in a Communist prison, being tortured for his faith. When he walked to the pulpit, I saw a little man, thin and emaciated, with hollowed out eyes and sunken in cheeks. But, when he talked, his face lit up with a radiant glow. As he told the story of his ministry in the underground church, God used his testimony to stir my heart. He has been with the Lord for several years now, but his voice is still speaking today. The impact of his testimony is still encouraging and motivating me and thousands of others who heard him speak. That is the kind of testimony I want to leave behind for the glory of God. But, I can only leave that testimony if I listen to His blood, His Word, and the testimony of other faithful believers. When you hear God speak, do not refuse Him. Do not turn away. Do not turn back. Obey His voice. Run to Him and find His will. Do His will and forever you will be blessed.

26. Why Does God Shake It Up?

"See that ye refuse not him that speaketh. For if they escaped not who refused him that spake on earth, much more shall not we escape, if we turn away from him that speaketh from heaven: Whose voice then shook the earth: but now he hath promised, saying, Yet once more I shake not the earth only, but also heaven. And this word, Yet once more, signifieth the removing of those things that are shaken, as of things that are made, that those things which cannot be shaken may remain." –Hebrews 12:25-27

Judgment for Those Who Refuse to Listen

It is an incredible privilege to have God speak to us through the blood of Jesus, through His Word, through His Holy Spirit, and through other believers. However, that privilege is joined with an awesome level of responsibility. The fact that God speaks to us means that we are going to be held responsible to take heed and not refuse His voice. Let's look at why this listening is so important.

First, those who did not listen to God's messengers could not escape the end result. As we saw at Mount Sinai, Moses received the Law of God for the people. God did not talk to the people; He only talked to Moses. Those who refused to listen and heed God's Word through Moses were destroyed. Hebrews 10:28 says, *"He that despised Moses' law died* *without mercy under two or three witnesses."* The law was literally a matter of life and death. Moses did not make the laws; he merely announced them, but he was announcing them on God's behalf. There was no means of escape, no mercy for those who refused to listen.

This statement would have had a special importance to the Hebrew Christians to whom this letter was originally written. They, like their ancestors before them, had been following and trying to keep the law for thousands of years. They knew the stories of what had happened to those who disobeyed. They knew the seriousness and significance of heeding Moses' words. They knew the terrible punishment on those who refused God's messenger.

But with many of them God was not well pleased: for they were overthrown in the wilderness. Now these things were our examples, to the intent we should not lust after evil things, as they also lusted. Neither be ye idolaters, as were some of them; as it is written, The people sat down to eat and drink, and rose up to play. Neither let us commit fornication as some of them committed, and fell in one day three and twenty thousand. Neither let us tempt Christ, as some of them also tempted, and were destroyed of serpents. Neither murmur ye, as some of them also murmured, and were destroyed of the destroyer. Now all these things happened unto them for ensamples: and they are written for our admonition, upon whom the ends of the world are come. (I Corinthians 10:5-11)

Judgment for Disobedience to God's Messengers

Second, those who disobey the voice of Heaven disobey the greatest authority. Often, we are tempted to excuse disobedience to God's messengers. "He's just a man. That's just his opinion." We see from this passage that those who did so in Moses' day paid for it with their lives. If the punishment for disobeying God's human messengers is so severe, imagine what the punishment for disobeying God's Word and His Spirit must be! When you read the Bible, you are reading a letter from your Creator. The still, small voice you have inside you is a big God—the Holy Spirit taking the words you read in Scripture and making personal application of them to your life. He can apply it to you because He knows everything about it, and He knows everything about you.

The very Sustainer of my life has chosen by His grace and His mercy to speak to me personally. The great King, the Saviour of all the redeemed, the Master of the Universe, cares enough to communicate with an insignificant speck like me! How could I ever refuse His voice when He speaks? Often, when we read the Bible, we fail to realize what we are doing. The Bible is not like the Sunday paper, a magazine, or a history book. It is the living Word of God. Because it is alive, the Word speaks to us in the present, active tense. It is a tragedy when we do not heed His voice to us through the Bible.

Judgment for Turning Your Back on God

Third, there is no greater insult than to turn away from the Lord Jesus when He is speaking. It is a sign of disrespect when you do not look at someone who is speaking to you. (It's also a sign of guilt when someone won't look you in the eye when you're talking to them.) The protocol of royalty is that you never turn your back on the king or queen. Instead, you walk backward out of their presence to avoid showing disrespect. Yet, the author of Hebrews indicates that people are turning away from the King of Kings. Very few people were even allowed into the presence of kings in Bible times. Esther told Mordecai that entering the throne room without permission could result in death. We have been given the privilege of listening to God Himself...and yet, sometimes, we turn it down because we do not want to hear what He has to say to us.

Is not our King worthy of having our eyes focused on Him and Him alone? Is He not deserving of the highest measure and level of respect? Should we not give the Bible the attention that it rightly deserves? Do not refuse God when He speaks to you. Jesus came to earth as the Lamb of God. He is going to return as the Lion of Judah. When John—who was the closest disciple to Jesus—saw Him in the Revelation, he fell on his face and could not speak. If we saw Jesus for who He really is, we would never disrespect Him by turning away from His voice. Through His Word and His Spirit, Jesus took time to talk to you today. Did you take time to listen to Him, or were you too busy preoccupied with something else?

To Demonstrate the Power of His Voice

Fourth, we should listen because of the immeasurable power of His voice. The sound of God's voice can shake the entire earth. This is a reference back to what happened at Mount Sinai. When God spoke, the mountain moved—the word used carries the idea of rocking or swaying, as would happen during an earthquake. The creation of the world was done by the voice of God. Throughout Genesis 1, we read, *"And God said...and it was so."* Hebrews 11:3 says, *"Through faith we understand that the worlds were framed by the word of God."* The only thing God made with his hands was man; everything else was spoken into existence. As well, the judgment at the end of the world will also be accomplished by the voice of God.

And I saw heaven opened, and behold a white horse; and he that sat upon him was called Faithful and True, and in righteousness he doth judge and make war. His eyes were as a flame of fire, and on his head were many crowns; and he had a name written, that no man knew, but he himself. And he was clothed with a vesture dipped in blood: and his name is called The Word of God. And the armies which were in heaven followed him upon white horses, clothed in fine linen, white and clean. And out of his mouth goeth a sharp sword, that with it he should smite the nations: and he shall rule them with a rod of iron: and he treadeth the winepress of the fierceness and wrath of Almighty God. (Revelation 19:11-15)*

Someone whose voice has that kind of power must be heeded. This is a prophecy for the future, but its significance for students in Adversity University is unmistakable. We get so busy and preoccupied, that we tend to ignore the most important voice of all—the voice of the Lord Jesus. But, it is imperative that we listen to His voice. Not only will God one day shake the earth and the heavens, but God also is shaking your life and mine through the adversity that He brings to get us to move beyond our comfort zone and grow in grace.

To Remove the Rubble from our Lives

Fifth, the voice of God removes the rubble from our lives if we heed it. Verse twenty-seven talks about "the removing of those things that are shaken."

When God shakes our world, it is not because He wants to hurt us; He is trying to help us. His purpose is to shake us up so that those things that do not belong in our lives will fall away. It is like the process the old miners used in panning for gold. They would dip the pan into water, and then swirl it around and around. Since the gold was heavier than the sand and dirt, it would settle to the bottom of the pan while the debris washed over the sides.

We are not inclined to release our grip on the things that are temporal, but we cannot grip that which is eternal unless we do. So, God shakes our world to loosen our grasp on everything but Him. Growth and advancement and maturity in Adversity University only come when we focus our hearts and set our priorities on the things of God. Adversity clarifies our vision and values. Jesus told Peter that Satan would sift him like wheat is sifted. (Luke 22:31) Why would God allow that to happen? The purpose of sifting is not to hurt the wheat; it is to remove the chaff. After the sifting, only those things that are important will remain. Oh, that we would learn this lesson!

God is too good to be bad to you. Sometimes, difficult things happen and you will say, "Oh, I don't know how I can go on." But, you must go on with God. He is shaking your world to remove those things that are keeping you back from maturing and growing spiritually. Moses is a perfect example of this. Moses was one of the most privileged men of his day. To be educated in Egypt was to receive the finest education available in the world. Raised in Pharaoh's household, Moses was trained and educated with the best of the best that was available in Egypt. Acts 7:22 reminds us, *"And Moses was learned in all the wisdom of the Egyptians, and was mighty in words and in deeds."* By the world's standards, he had everything he needed to be a great leader, but God was not impressed, so He shook Moses' world.

Moses killed the Egyptian overseer who was beating a Hebrew slave and fled to the desert. For forty years, God sifted him. Before Moses was ready to serve God and lead Israel, he had to let go of some things he had learned. By the time he met God at the burning bush, Moses had lost all of his self-confidence and self-reliance. Before he had thought that people should look to him, now he did not think he could be a leader. Moses was not ready until he realized that only God could do the work, and that God would work through him. God wants to shake our world, because He wants to remove that which will hinder us from glorifying Him and living our lives fully dependent upon Him by faith.

This is one of the reasons even mature believers still find their worlds shaken. We all tend, as we grow and mature, to become independent of God. We begin to think, "I don't need God; I can go my own way and get by on my own." We do not say that out loud, but we begin neglecting our devotional life, and we begin neglecting church. So, God shakes our world again. His purpose is to remove those things that need to fall away in order that He might use us. When we are shaken, all that remains will be that which brings honor and glory to Him. It is after we are shaken that our character develops, so we can be useful to the Lord and to others.

27. BE A SEA OF GALILEE CHRISTIAN – NOT A DEAD SEA DUD!

"Wherefore we receiving a kingdom which cannot be moved, let us have grace, whereby we may serve God acceptably with reverence and godly fear: For our God is a consuming fire."—Hebrews 12:28-29

Student and Servant

We have been talking about our role as students in Adversity University, but these verses tell us that we are not only students, but we have also been called to be servants. God's plan is for us to serve while we study. While I was still in school, my parents helped me get a job at the Cool Farm Dairy down the road from our house. I would ride the bus home from school, change clothes, and then get on my bicycle and ride to work. I helped carry groceries out for people. I was a student, but I had a job. When I went off to Bible college, I worked at a service station. (Young people today have no idea what a service station is.) When people pulled in, I would go out, find out how much gas they wanted, and pump it for them. I would check the fluid in the radiator, check the oil, check the tires, and make sure everything was working like it should. I even washed the windshield for them. Even though I was a student, I always had a job.

God does not intend for us just to sit back and learn; He expects us to be working at the same time. We are not just enrolled in school to study about God and His Word and learn how to love Him; we are also to serve God with our lives. In fact if you do not serve God, your studies are going to be very dull and boring. People who do not serve are the most likely to drop out of Adversity University. Why? It is because they are like the Dead Sea.

I learned about the Dead Sea from Mr. Smith, my 5th and 6th grade Sunday School teacher. I still remember him drawing a map of Israel on the chalkboard of our classroom. Toward the top, he drew the Sea of Galilee. Then, he drew the Jordan River flowing south down to the Dead Sea. He labeled the Mediterranean Sea, Syria, and the mountains of the region. He showed us where Jesus was baptized by John and where Jerusalem, Bethlehem, and Nazareth are. Then, he told us about the Dead Sea. The salt content of the Dead Sea is more than eight times higher than it is in the oceans. In fact, it is so high that if you sit in the water, you will not sink! Now, if you visit the Sea of Galilee, you will see lots of people fishing. But, you never see that at the Dead Sea. No one has fishing lines or nets out in the water. Nothing lives in the water. I remember Mr. Smith telling us, "The Sea of Galilee has fresh water coming in, and it has fresh water coming out. The Dead Sea has fresh water coming in, but it has no outlet."

He said, "Boys, it's a good thing to get to know God's Word and to get to know Him, but God also wants us to serve Him with our lives. The only way we can stay fresh is when we're both taking in and giving out." That is why, at the end of Hebrews 12, God emphasizes our service to Him. He wants us to be a Sea of Galilee Christian and not a Dead Sea dud. Every believer is called to serve God acceptably with no exceptions. Service is not just for preachers and missionaries and Christian school teachers. Every believer is included in the call of Romans 12:1-2 to present our bodies to God to serve Him.

Do Not Just Stay in the Classroom

When I was sixteen, Romans 12 started to work in my life. It became more than words on a page; it became reality. On a Friday night, God moved in my heart, and I said, "I surrender all. I do not know what You are going to have me do with my life, but I want to do whatever You want me to do." When I began to serve God, church services took on a whole new meaning to me. What I was learning on Sunday, I was implementing in my life all through that week in my service to God. My pastor helped me get started preaching at the Rescue Mission and at the jail. When I went off to college, I took classes, and worked all week. But, on Sundays, I was working in a local New Testament church serving God. All through my life, I have not only had the privilege of being a student in Adversity University, but I have had the privilege of being a servant of the Lord. I want to be a Sea of Galilee Christian, not a Dead Sea dud.

So often I have seen this pattern. God teaches us a lesson in school, and then He reinforces it by giving us the opportunity for using that lesson to help someone else. God is equipping you for a life of service. Can you imagine a cooking class that only used books and never took the students into a kitchen? Would a medical school ever let a doctor graduate who had never been in the operating room? It takes more than just academic knowledge to be prepared. You do not become a good athlete by reading about running; you have to get out on the track and practice running. God never intended for students in Adversity University to just be in the classroom and not be out serving Him.

Most of the dropouts from Adversity University are Dead Sea duds. They take in the preaching and teaching of the Word of God. They learn principles through teaching and testing. They go through adversity, but they never use what they have learned. They take in, but they do not give out. If you want to serve God, do the best you can to help others right where you are. Serving God is not for the future (for after graduation) – after all, graduation from Adversity University is not going to happen until you reach Heaven – it is for right now. If you want to serve God, then be the best husband or wife you can be; be the best employee where you work; be the best friend to people who are hurting. If you do not focus on serving God, you will find yourself disappointed in serving people.

If you are focused on people, you are going to be hurt when things do not turn out the way you think they should. Years ago, Dr. Bill Rice, who founded the Bill Rice Ranch ministry, helped a pastor who had lost his church. The man was a Southern Baptist, who had been somewhat critical of Dr. Rice as an independent Baptist, but he still offered to help. After the man lived at the Ranch for several months, receiving free housing and food, he got another job as a pastor. Because his new church was also Southern Baptist, he started criticizing Dr. Rice again. Dr. Bill Rice's son asked him why he had helped a man who was so critical of him. Dr. Rice replied, "I didn't do it for him. I did it for the Lord."

Have an Outlet for Service

Being a student in Adversity University is tough. The classes are hard. We may be tempted to pull back from service, but that is the route to becoming a Dead Sea dud. If you don't have an outlet for service, then you are going to lose the freshness, the vitality, and the joy that comes from serving God *while* you're studying God. The two go hand in hand. In Acts 6, we see the problems that came with the growth of the early church. The Jewish widows were being cared for, but the Grecian widows were not. The Apostles asked for a group of men to be selected to care for those needs, so that they could stay focused on preaching the Gospel and studying the Word. Notice that they did not just pick anybody; they wanted wise, honest, and Spirit-filled men. (Acts 6:3) They were going to serve tables, but they were really serving God.

Some people say, "It doesn't matter how I live, as long as I'm just busy serving God." It does matter. Ladies in the nursery changing diapers need to be filled with the Holy Spirit. Men working in the factory making tools need to be filled with the Holy Spirit. Every Christian in every walk of life needs to be living right and serving others. Every student in Adversity University is also called to serve God acceptably at home, at church, in business, and everywhere. Jesus said that the one is greatest is the one who is the servant. (Matthew 23:11) Many people want the blessings and benefits without paying the price of serving. Most people would be willing to start out as the CEO; not many are willing to be the janitor. You will be amazed what opportunities God gives you if you faithfully serve Him right where you are.

In 1974, just two days before I got married, Pastor Alley of North Love Baptist Church asked to meet with Dianne and me. We met him and his family at a restaurant in Kalamazoo, Michigan. Dianne and I knew we were supposed to get married, but we weren't sure where God was going to lead us to serve Him. We were stunned and shocked when Pastor Alley said, "Paul, I want you to know the church has voted, and we want you to come and be the youth pastor." Why did they ask me? Because when I first started coming to North Love, I was willing to do anything and everything he asked me to do. I did not have an attitude about it, no matter what it was. I just wanted to serve God. What happens when we serve Him with a willing spirit?

Serve Him with a Willing Spirit

First, **we receive a kingdom that cannot be moved**. Throughout the Bible, we see references to the kingdom of God or the kingdom of Heaven. This kingdom is the inheritance of every child of God. And as we go through our schooling, and as we struggle with adversity and focus on serving others, we should always have in mind the eternal future that has been promised to us. There is a permanent position waiting for us when we are finished with school. Earthly kingdoms are temporary. They come and go. Nothing moves or changes the kingdom of Heaven. It is settled and eternal. No economic collapse, no military attack, and no sickness will ever threaten that perfect place. Keeping the coming kingdom in mind is vital, because what we do here influences what happens there.

Jesus told parable after parable about servants whose masters went away, leaving them to work while He was gone. Those servants, who were diligent and faithful, received rewards for their service. Those who were lazy and mistreated their fellow servants were condemned and judged. The Bible teaches that there are rewards in Heaven based on our service on earth. I want God to say, "Well done." I want to know that I have done my very best for Him. I want there to be an excellent position for me in His Kingdom. Those who receive the rewards are those who pay the price by serving God in obscurity, serving God when it does not feel good, (by the way…it will never feel good) serving God whether your ministry expands or gets smaller.

Serve Him through His Grace

Second, **we serve God through His grace**. That is how Jesus served His Father. Hebrews 2:9 says, *"That he by the grace of God should taste death for every man."* The only way you and I can serve God acceptably is by His grace. Grace is the desire and the ability to be and do what God calls us to be and do. Grace is the fuel of the Christian life. If your car is out of gas, you can get some people to push it and make it move, but it is not running as it was meant to run. The Christian life only runs on grace. Nothing else will substitute for it. You can try to do it on your own, but you are going to get tired and drop out.

Paul had a thorn in his flesh (II Corinthians 12:7)—some physical malady that made his life miserable. You can find lots of preachers today (the kind you shouldn't be listening to) who will tell you God wants everything in your life to be perfect. That is not what the Bible says. Paul prayed for his thorn to be removed, but God refused. God told Paul that it was part of his training; that he needed the thorn to keep from being proud. What God said instead was, *"My grace is sufficient for thee: for my strength is made perfect in weakness."* (II Corinthians 12:9) God's grace equips us to serve Him. It is only through that grace, that we can rise above and overcome the adversities that we face during our race.

Serve Him with Reverence and Fear

Third, **we serve God with reverence and fear**. God doesn't accept irreverent service. He requires us to revere Him while we are serving Him. Unfortunately, we often find ourselves serving God; not revering Him, but resenting Him. When I think of the importance of serving God with reverence, I think of the story of Nadab and Abihu. As the sons of Aaron, they were supposed to help their father in the worship and service of God. Instead, they violated the rules of service, and God struck them dead with fire. (Leviticus 10:1-3) Serving God is serious business that requires us to reverence Him.

God also says that we are to serve Him with fear. Sometimes, we are tempted to say, "Well, as long as I'm serving God, it doesn't matter what

I'm doing in the off hours." There are no off hours in the Christian life. Many people who claim to be serving God are really serving themselves and their flesh instead. How many prominent Christian leaders have been revealed to be hypocrites? They stood and preached the Word, but they did not follow their own preaching. Men who fear God do not live that way.

Perhaps you have heard the true story behind the contemporary Christian song "The Healer." For two years, Michael Guglielmucci performed the song, telling people that he had written it during his battle with terminal cancer. Often, he appeared on stage with oxygen. The song rapidly climbed up the charts, and a video of it on You Tube drew over 400,000 hits in just a few days. Then, the truth came out. The whole story was a lie. Guglielmucci never had cancer. All of the sympathy he received and the donations people sent him were based on a complete falsehood. It is a great privilege to serve our God, and that privilege must be taken seriously. If you are not serving Him with reverence and godly fear, you are not really serving Him at all. And if you do not serve Him, you will end up as lifeless and barren as the Dead Sea.

28. Consuming Fire

"Wherefore we receiving a kingdom which cannot be moved, let us have grace, whereby we may serve God acceptably with reverence and godly fear: For our God is a consuming fire." —Hebrews 12:28-29

Intense Flames

When I was young, one of my best friends, Robert, lived in Battle Creek, Michigan. We lived in Kalamazoo. There was no interstate between the two towns. If we were going to visit them, we had to take a little two lane highway—US 94. It has been some forty-five years now; but I will never forget one Saturday afternoon, when we were on our way to their house. It was a bright, sunny day; but as we came to the top of a hill, we saw a pillar of thick smoke rising into the sky. We knew from the smoke and the smell in the air that there was a fire in the wreckage ahead of us, but we could not see it. My father pulled over to the side of the road, and he and I went to see if we could do something to help.

A car in front of us had hit an eighteen wheeler. We found out later that this car hit the truck as it tried to pass another car. As we approached the wreck, we saw that the driver of the truck was trapped inside the tangled, burning wreckage. I heard him screaming for help as flames got closer and closer to him. I have never heard anyone make a sound like that before or since. It was heartbreaking. There was nothing we could do to help him. The flames were too intense. He continued to scream until the gas tank exploded, then he went out into eternity. I have never forgotten that day. I want you to read these words very carefully: Yes, our God is love; but our God is also a consuming fire.

God has enrolled us in Adversity University not just for our own development, but so that we can serve Him. Serving God is serious business; and according to the Bible, we must serve Him acceptably— acceptably according to His definition, not ours. In the last chapter, we examined the concept of serving God with reverence and fear. God commands and demands that we serve Him with our lives. He is a God of love and grace and mercy. However, He is more than just that, and we cannot forget His holiness and justice. If we take what we have learned as students in Adversity University and do not serve God acceptably, then everything He has brought about in our lives is wasted. Remember, it is about more than just our development. There is a world around us that desperately needs His help. So, let's look at the aspects of God's nature that are described by calling Him a consuming fire, and the implications for our service.

God Consumes Unconverted

First, **God will consume the unconverted.** Make no mistake about it; death is not simply the end of existence for the unsaved. There is a place, a very real place, for every man and woman who dies without Jesus Christ as his or her personal Saviour. Hell is a place. It is not a state of mind or a figment of imagination. Outside the city of Jerusalem in Jesus' day was a dump called Gehenna. They burned trash there, with the fire never going out. That is the visual Jesus used to describe the eternal place of judgment for the unconverted.

In Luke 16:24, the rich man in Hell said, *"Father Abraham, have mercy on me, and send Lazarus, that he may dip the tip of his finger in water and cool my tongue; for I am tormented in this flame."*

All of the people you and I rub shoulders with each and every day will spend eternity somewhere. Every one of them is either saved or unsaved. Those who are unsaved need someone to tell them the gospel. Yet, so many Christians are ashamed of the Saviour. They are not willing to be a witness to the truth. They never serve God by telling others about salvation in Jesus Christ. God has enrolled us in Adversity University to equip and prepare us to be effective evangelists. If we do not serve God and do not fulfill our responsibility to warn a lost and dying world of eternal judgment, then how will they hear? (Romans 10:14)

When we are tempted to be silent, we need to remember God's consuming fire.

Jude 23 says it this way, *"And others save with fear, pulling them out of the fire; hating even the garment spotted by the flesh."* It is our responsibility, our privilege, and our reasonable service to be a witness to this lost and dying world. God is a God of grace and mercy, but once someone travels through the valley of the shadow of death, there is no purgatory—there is no second chance. All who die without Christ as their Saviour go to Hell forever. Our God is a consuming fire. My service or my lack of service for God will make an eternal difference in someone else's life. I urge you to serve God with your life. What God has done to redeem and transform your life, He will do for others. They need to hear the Good News.

Romans 1:16 says, *"For I am not ashamed of the gospel of Christ: for it is the power of God unto salvation to every one that believeth; to the Jew first, and also to the Greek."* God has called every one of us to be His witnesses. Our coursework at Adversity University is designed to help us be better at this crucial task. Think about the person who brought you the gospel message. If they had the same level of dedication of serving God that you do, would you know Jesus today? God is a consuming fire, and He will consume the wicked and remove them from His presence forever and ever.

God Consumes Obstacles

Second, **God will consume anything that keeps us from serving Him**. The first time fire is mentioned in the Bible is in the story of the destruction of the cities of Sodom and Gomorrah. Those cities did not have to be destroyed. It is true that they were very wicked, but the thing that ultimately caused the destruction of Sodom and Gomorrah was not sodomy; it was the sin of Lot, the one saved man in the city. Second, Peter chapter two tells us that Lot was a righteous man, and that he hated the sin of Sodom. Lot was a like many of us. He did not like what was going on in his society. The tragedy is that he did not do anything about it. God told Abraham that if He found just ten righteous people in Sodom, He would spare the city. Because Lot was not willing to serve God, the cities were destroyed.

If Lot had seen to it that his own family was saved—his wife, his married daughters and his sons-in-law, his grandchildren, and his single daughters—there would have been enough righteous people to spare Sodom. Instead, most of Lot's family was destroyed in the fire and brimstone. And even though Lot and two of his daughters escaped, their story also had a tragic end.

Our Responsibility

Your decision to serve God has a direct impact on where you live. The biggest problem in the Unites States of America today is not the Democrats or the Republicans or the Independents. Our problem is not in San Francisco or Las Vegas or New York City or Washington or New Orleans. The greatest problem in America is found in our fundamental, Bible-believing, Baptist churches. It is good to go to church, but that is not enough. God's purpose for our lives is for us to serve Him. That is why we are here.

The second time fire is mentioned in the Bible is in the story of Abraham offering his son, Isaac. Abraham waited for years for Isaac to be born. He loved his son, the child of his old age. God said to Abraham, "Abraham, I'm going to ask you to do something that's really unusual. There is someone coming in between you and me. Someone is becoming more important to you than I am. He is going to hinder you from serving me effectively. I want you to take your son Isaac up to a mountain and offer him as a sacrifice." Genesis 22:6 tells us that Abraham took fire with him for the burnt offering. The mountain they went to was the same mountain where Jesus was crucified for our sins. Abraham took his son there, fully intending to take his son's life by offering him as a sacrifice to God.

Complete Sacrifice

Abraham understood this principle: Anyone or anything that takes precedence over God in our lives will be consumed with fire. God will remove it from its position for His glory and for our good. When you are tempted to say "No" to God and hold on to something that comes between you and Him, remember that He is a consuming fire. He is committed to burning the dross out of our lives, so that we might come forth as gold, pure and refined for His glory. The statement that God is a consuming fire is actually a quote from Deuteronomy 4:24, which says, *"For the Lord thy God is a consuming fire, even a jealous God."* God does not want anything or anyone to take His place in our lives. This is a stern warning to not allow anything to keep us from serving Him.

Cost of Disobedience

Moses was speaking to the people from painful experience. This verse is found in the recounting of the story of Moses striking the rock to bring forth water in disobedience to God's command. As a result of his defiance, God declared that Moses would not be allowed to enter the Promised Land. Moses served God for many years, but there was one point in his life when he lost his reverence and fear for God and stopped serving Him. The cost for that disobedience was very high. So, in Deuteronomy 4, Moses is begging the people not to tell God "No." What Moses did (Numbers 20)—striking the rock instead of speaking to it—seems to us like a very small thing. This story highlights for us the importance of serving God acceptably by His standards.

The people were complaining about a lack of water, and Moses was angry at them. As a result, he did not obey God. Water came out of the rock; the people's needs were met. But, Moses would rue that day for the rest of his life.

Do you know why what he did was such a big deal? Do you know why God punished Moses so harshly according to our way of thinking? It was because he left God out. It is that simple. Moses said to the people, "Must Aaron and I fetch you water out of this rock?" Because of what Moses did, he got the glory instead of God. God is a jealous God, and He is a consuming fire.

Whack! Whack! God sent the water, and everybody said, "That Moses, he's a great guy." God said, "No Moses, I'm a jealous God; and now these people, they think you did it, and I don't get the glory from it, and I am not going to sit idly by and let you serve Me without reverence and godly fear." Our God is a consuming fire.

Stay in School and Graduate with Honors

I was one of a group of teenagers in my home church who dedicated our lives to serving God. Even as young people, we were active and involved and doing what we could in the church. Most of us went to Bible college to complete training for our service to Him. But, one of our friends decided to stay home instead. Though he loved God and was involved in the church, he had made some friends at the public high school, and he followed them away from the Lord. He lost his interest in church, and he started going out and doing drugs with his friends. Our junior year of college, Dianne's brother, David, and I were home for a break when this boy's mother called asking us to go visit him. She was heartbroken over the way he was living; and she hoped that as old friends of his, we might be able to reach him and bring him back to God.

We went to an apartment in a very bad part of town. We had not seen this young man in three years. I still remember how he used to play in the orchestra at church, using his talents to serve God. We knocked on the door and walked into a room with no furniture except an old stained mattress on the floor. There was garbage all around the room and a bare light bulb hanging from the ceiling. Our friend was sitting on that mattress. He could not even put a sentence together. He was not high; it was the toll of all the drugs he had taken over the years. They had ruined his brain. You may think that even though God has called you to serve Him, it is not that big a deal, and you can put it off. I beg you to remember that God is a consuming fire. Serve Him reverently and with fear. Serve Him now!

Throughout this book, we have looked at God's plan for your life. And, I want to close with this encouragement. God never makes a mistake. He knew exactly what He was doing when He planned your studies at Adversity University. Your heavenly Father has custom-designed your curriculum. He knows what you need; He knows what you can take. There will be days when you will struggle and wonder if you can make it; and yes, by His grace you can make it. You can receive a good report. There will be days when you will wonder if it is worth it; and yes, graduation day is coming. Stay in school; do not drop out. Keep your eyes on Jesus. Run with patience and finish the race. And when you do, you will become a person of great faith. Your picture will join the many others in the hall of graduates, and your life will inspire others to see that you have graduated with honors. They will follow you and learn from your endurance in Adversity University.

About the Author

 Dr. Paul Kingsbury is the senior pastor of North Love Baptist Church in Rockford, Illinois. Under his leadership, the congregation has grown to nine hundred regularly attending members. Pastor Kingsbury's shepherding heart for his people and their church is outreach of the lost and development of those to whom God has called him to lead. The church has many ministries including North Love Christian School and North Love Baptist Bible Institute.

Perhaps the most extraordinary aspect of Dr. Kingsbury's ministry is the birth of Reformers Unanimous, a local church-based addictions program. From a small Bible study twelve years ago, Reformers Unanimous is now being used in more than five hundred churches across the United States and several other countries around the world. Thousands of people have found freedom and victory in Christ out of serious addictive behaviors through this program. Pastor Kingsbury's church has also opened discipleship homes for men and women, where they may be discipled from a lifestyle of stubborn habits to developing a personal relationship with Jesus Christ.

Dr. Kingsbury has been privileged to preach across the United States and in more than two dozen foreign countries in his thirty-six years of ministry. Pastor Kingsbury received honorary doctorates from Ambassador Baptist College in May of 2003 and West Coast Baptist College in 2006.

Dr. Kingsbury and his wife Dianne have twelve children and four grandchildren, all of whom are serving Christ with their lives.

More Books from Dr. Paul Kingsbury

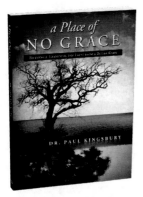

A Place of No Grace
Bitterness: Examining the Fruit from a Bitter Root

A Place of No Grace is an exciting new book by Pastor Paul Kingsbury. This insightful book gives an in-depth analysis of bitterness: the causes, the effects, and the treatment of this catastrophic condition. This book makes an excellent gift for: RU students, church members, and family.

#PK-100 **$9.00**

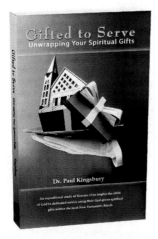

Gifted to Serve
Unwrapping Your Spiritual Gifts

Have you ever wondered what God's purpose is for you? Have you ever felt like parts of your ministry are satisfying while others are not? Are you seeking true fulfillment in your life and in your ministry? If you answered "yes" to any of these questions, then this book is for you. *Gifted to Serve* is an expositional study of Romans 12, written to inspire the child of God to dedicated service using their God-given spiritual gifts within the local New Testament church. By helping you determine and use your unique spiritual gift mix, you will find new fulfillment in your life and ministry.

#RB-108 **$15.00**

Reformers Unanimous Material

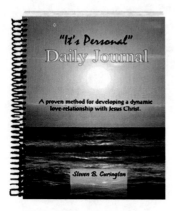

#CE-111 $15.00

"It's Personal" Daily Journal
Classic Size

RU looking for a devotional tool that's more than a glorified notebook? Discover the revolutionary tool that has helped many individuals walk and talk with Christ and have a victorious Christian life. The 90-day *"It's Personal"* Daily Journal is a proven method for developing a dynamic love-relationship with Jesus Christ. This journal is our #1 selling product in America! It comes complete with an instructional CD explaining how to use the journal and its five forms of communication in order to maximize your personal walk with God.

(7x 8.5 size, 90 -day supply, Includes instructional CD)

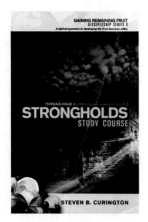

#CE-103 $15.00

Strongholds Study Course
Gaining Remaining Fruit Discipleship Series I

This book represents your first book, the Strongholds Study Course. It is followed by the Uphold and Behold Study Courses. These three workbooks represent the entire GRF Discipleship Course. It is available, as shown here for adults, and has also been developed for teens and young children as well. No matter your age or struggle, the GRF Discipleship Series can help you know God in a more personal and intimate manner.

reformu.com or 815-986-0460

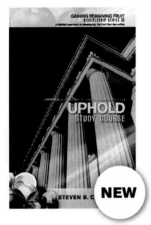

#CE-203 **$20.00**

Uphold Study Course
Gaining Remaining Fruit Discipleship Series **II**

This book represents your second book, the Upholds Study Course. It is preceded by the Strongholds and followed by the Behold Study Courses. These three workbooks represent the entire GRF Discipleship Course. It is available, as shown here for adults, and it has been developed for teens and young children as well. No matter your age or struggle, the GRF Discipleship Series can help you know God in a more personal and intimate manner.

COMING SOON!

#CE-303 **$20.00**

Behold Study Course
Gaining Remaining Fruit Discipleship Series **III**

This book represents your third book, the Behold Study Course. It is preceded by the Strongholds and Uphold Study Courses. These three workbooks represent the entire GRF Discipleship Course. It is available, as shown here for adults, and it has been developed for teens and young children as well. No matter your age or struggle, the GRF Discipleship Series can help you know God in a more personal and intimate manner.

GRF I, II, III
Gaining Remaining Fruit Discipleship Series
Complete Set

#CE-403 **$49.00**

reformu.com or 815-986-0460